The Solar House

The Solar House

A guide to solar energy utilisation in domestic, industrial and commercial building

P. R. Sabady, Dip.Arch (EAUG/SIA)

Translated by P. A. Cummins, CEng, MIEE
Edited by I. F. R. Dickinson, CEng, MRAeS, BSc

NEWNES-BUTTERWORTHS

LONDON · BOSTON
Sydney · Wellington · Durban · Toronto

THE BUTTERWORTH GROUP

United Kingdom
Butterworth & Co (Publishers) Ltd
London: 88 Kingsway, WC2B 6AB

Australia
Butterworths Pty Ltd
Sydney: 586 Pacific Highway, Chatswood, NSW 2067
Also at Melbourne, Brisbane, Adelaide and Perth

Canada
Butterworth & Co (Canada) Ltd
Toronto: 2265 Midland Avenue, Scarborough, Ontario M1P 4S1

New Zealand
Butterworths of New Zealand Ltd
Wellington: 77—85 Customhouse Quay, 1, CPO Box 472

South Africa
Butterworth & Co (South Africa) (Pty) Ltd
Durban: 152—154 Gale Street

USA
Butterworth (Publishers) Inc
Boston: 10 Tower Office Park, Woburn, Mass. 01801

First published in English, 1978
    Reprinted 1978, 1979

ISBN 0 408 00290 5

Typeset by Butterworths Litho Preparation Department
Printed in Great Britain at the University Press, Cambridge

Preface

The use of solar energy for heating purposes is now recognised and accepted by both technical experts and the general public. Although known for many decades in the past this technology came into prominence after the international oil crisis of 1973 when there was a world-wide demand for alternative sources of energy. Today many countries are constructing buildings specifically designed to use solar power so that these can be evaluated and operating data obtained.

This book is a translation of the well-known *Haus und Sonnenkraft* which is now in its third edition only a few months after publication. It is intended to be a reference manual for architects, builders and heating engineers and also to be of interest to the general reader.

In addition to the history and economic policy of the principles of solar energy, the problem of utilising the sun's radiation is examined from the viewpoint of the architect. The book describes and compares the different types of sun collector and analyses the many different storage methods which can be adopted. A separate chapter is devoted to solar buildings already in use in both Europe and the USA. The construction of these installations is fully described and technical performance data relating to them are given.

The text is concise and easily understandable. Numerous photographs, line diagrams and tables help the reader to obtain a clear concept of the past, present and future uses of solar energy.

Dedicated to Nora, Leila and Oliver

I Thank Nora, my wife, for her help.
My special thanks are due also to many others
for their guidance

Contents

Introduction

In November 1973, the energy crisis came almost unexpectedly, and western civilisation was placed for the first time under an energy embargo. Vehicles, factories and central heating systems threatened to come to a standstill, and we suddenly noticed that our energy-hungry consumer society is built on not very solid foundations.

Today we have oil once more, although we must pay much

Solar House in France by J. Michel (1975) (photo: P. Sabady)

more for it, but the world will never again be as it was before November 1973.

An increasing fear for energy reserves and for our standard of living dominates the world today. To waste energy has become a sin and new forms of energy supply are being sought. In magazines and on T.V. one sees pictures of unusual looking buildings which use radiation from the sun as their energy supply. As a result of this, one has the feeling that the use of solar energy for domestic purposes is quite new — something that was never there before. However, one forgets that the use of solar energy is a science thousands of years old, which was rediscovered in our century. Up to the present, new discoveries in the field of solar energy have chiefly been published only in specialised journals or in papers sponsored by universities, which are read only by comparatively

Top: Solar house with direct heating panels in France (Sofee)

Bottom: Semi-direct solar heating system in New Mexico (Baer)

few people. In this book it is hoped to provide information of general interest and to demonstrate to non-scientists the possibilities which exist for heating buildings from solar energy.

The use of oil may ultimately be restricted to the manufacture of vital raw materials and even proteins. It may be that the banning of oil for heating purposes is not far off and that this could be done, not on political grounds, but on those of common-sense.

We must understand that waste of energy and its associated pollution of the environment could destroy our whole civilisation, and that we need 'clean' energy. The realisation of this applies to engineers and scientists, architects, builders and politicians. All of us must recognise our responsibility and help to find a solution. This book offers a direct contribution towards the realisation of a better environment with more sun, and less pollution.

1 The Energy Problem

When we use the word 'energy' we think mainly of something abstract and technical, which is only for engineers and scientists. If we take a little time to think about it, we see that the history of Man was and is still a story of the struggle to obtain increasing amounts of energy. All the material achievements of Man were, in reality, new forms of energy supply and use. From time immemorial Man has needed energy to justify being able to work with a lesser application of strength, and to create more comfort for himself.

In the past, as soon as a new form of energy was discovered, Man's way of life changed and, after a short time, the daily life of the era was marked by the new form of energy. Man's very first form of energy was his own muscle power. He had to try to increase the effect of this power as he could only demand as much comfort as he was able to produce with his own hands. Thousands of years passed before Man succeeded in controlling the first extraneous energy — fire and the strength of tamed animals. The significance of these two forms of energy for Man is immeasurable. Even in the year 1860, 15 % of all energy used throughout the world was produced by human effort and 73 % by animal power.

Energy is used in the form of heat or as mechanical power. The first mechanical energy was produced by wind or water and not until much later by the conversion of heat or by means of detonation. Archimedes and Heron of Alexandria were the first to create mechanical power from heat.

The higher demand for energy came after a wish for a relatively more highly developed civilisation. We only need to think of the great heated bath complexes of ancient times. The installation in Tell-Asmar built about 300 B.C. was 55 m X 32 m. The palace of the king of Arzawa in S.W. Anatolia (1200 B.C.) had central floor heating installed. The Roman baths were heated with hot air and consumed a lot of energy. The Caracalla thermal baths were built for 2300 persons and those of Diocletia for 3200. All these installations served either Kings or the people as a whole. Never before had it been possible to provide such a large private supply of energy for so many people.

In the USA 6 % of the world population uses one third of the world production of energy. An American uses on an average three times as much energy as a West European, and nine times as much as a Turk. The adventure of modern energy began in the 17th century, when, at the time of the Renaissance the long

1

forgotten knowledge of Archimedes and Heron was rediscovered. The Frenchman Denis Papin was the first to build a steam installation. The 18th and mainly 19th centuries produced a long line of inventors and thinkers who created the intellectual and technical basis of our present day society.

An increasing number of machines were invented and made which, whilst allowing more luxury, naturally, needed more energy. Coal was the main source of energy up to 1958 but the progress of the last 20 years would have been inconceivable without oil -- first found at the beginning of the 19th century. A member of the Russian Academy of Sciences in St. Petersburg in 1906 announced: 'Oil is a useless excretion of the earth. It is a sticky fluid which stinks, and cannot be used in any way.' Since then altogether 38 billion (10^9) tonnes of oil have been used, and from 1955 to 1968 alone the oil consumption was tripled.

Today 5 billion tons of oil are used every year, and the experts reckon an annual increase of 7.3 %. The known petroleum reserves of our earth are estimated at 90 billion tons, which means that in about 45 years time not a drop of oil will remain. As the supply of oil decreases, the price of oil could be so high that the use of this source of energy for heating purposes will no longer be possible in practice.

What is the position with other sources of energy?

1.1 Coal

Reserves of coal are still fairly large, mainly in the Soviet Union, the USA and China. Experts estimate that these amount to 7600 billion tons, and that coal will reach its maximum use about the year 2150 and not become scarce until the year 2300. Coal was also the first source of energy to bring about protection of the environment. In 1307 all lime kilns in London using coal were forbidden on account of the heavy production of smoke. The extraction of coal is getting more difficult; fifty years ago the depth was 350 m, today the average depth is from 700 to 1000 m. The daily extraction lays waste many square kilometres of countryside.

1.2 Atomic energy

This is one of the greatest hopes of our century. Already in America 5 %, and in Europe 1 %, of the energy requirements are met from atomic sources. According to the forecast of the UNO Atomic Energy Agency, 70 % of the world requirements in the year 2000 should be met from atomic energy. It is estimated that by 1985, atomic energy will provide in the USA 16.7 % of requirements; France 50 %, Germany 25 % and the UK 7 %. However, the unsolved technical problems are very great, and many theoretical results cannot yet be put into practice. The Deuterium-Tritium fusion reactor, in which the same fusion processes take place as in the sun, has been under study since 1952, but the problem does not look like being solved before the year 2000.

The difficulties and dangers of the production of atomic energy are well-known from the many discussions in the media of all countries. The main problem is that our scientists, seventy-seven years after the discovery of the first radioactive elements, still do not know how to dispose of the radioactive waste, and what should become of the reactor buildings when they have ceased operating. If these problems find no economic or ecological solution, the price of atomic energy will be so high, that the reckoning will reach immeasurable heights, not only for the undeveloped countries, but for the rich Western countries. It is to be hoped that a solution will be found for these pressing problems, otherwise the dreamed of Atomic Age could end before it begins, and atomic research would go into human history as the most mistaken investment of our civilisation.

1.3 Other forms of energy

The other classical forms of energy such as water power (5 % in 1975, approximately 2 % in 1985) and natural gas (reserves for about 50 years) are only available at present in limited quantities. These can, therefore, provide only a small part of our future energy requirements.

For some time the experts have known about this less satisfactory aspect of our energy economy, but it was only brought into the open by the oil crisis of 1973. So perhaps the oil embargo has even now brought us more of value than the cheap flood of oil of the last fifteen years.

In fact, we seem to be fortunate that through the increase in the price of oil, research into new pollution-free energy has been intensified, and at last governments and private industry are ready to make larger sums available for research into alternative sources of energy. At present wind energy, geothermal, biological gas and other forms of energy are being examined, but our largest and cleanest energy source lies 149 million km away — the Sun.

2 The Sun as a Source of Energy

The 'carrier' of solar energy is radiation; it consists of visible light radiation and invisible ultra-violet and infra-red radiation (Figure 2.1). Visible light has a wavelength from $0.4\,\mu$ to $0.8\,\mu$ ($1\,\mu = 10^{-6}$ m), ultra-violet is shorter than $0.4\,\mu$ and infra-red longer than $0.8\,\mu$. About 9 % of the sun's radiation lies in the band of heat radiation. The sun, a glowing sphere of gas, consists mainly of hydrogen (70 %) and helium (27 %). Energy is created as a result of nuclear transformation. In this way the sun loses a million tons of its mass in every second. The radiation intensity at the sun's surface amounts to between 70 000 and 80 000 kW/m² at a temperature of 6000°C. Our earth receives only a small, but significant part of this amount of power, namely; approximately 180 000 billion kW. This is about 18 000 times more than the amount which Man has up to now produced altogether on the earth.

Outside the earth's atmosphere, the flow of radiation still amounts to 1394 W/m² or 2.0 cal/cm² min. This value is called the *Solar Constant*. In passing through the atmosphere a large part of this radiation is absorbed (30—40 %) so that the earth's surface at sea level on a clear day receives between 0.855 kW/m² and 1.00 kW/m² of direct radiation. Naturally, a part (about 50 %) of the diffuse radiation in the atmosphere reaches the earth's surface in the form of energy.

The duration of sunshine and the intensity of the radiation are locally dependent on the time of year, the weather conditions and of course the geographical position. About 25 % of the earth's surface has sunshine all day, i.e. direct solar radiation. In most countries the duration of sunshine and radiation intensity have been measured for decades. For solar engineering calculations year-long average values are available for each hour of the day and for each month. Values are also determined for horizontal and variously oriented vertical surfaces. From this data it is possible to obtain the appropriate value of the radiation effect for each hour of the day.

2.1 Direct radiation

This is the radiation which we simply call sunshine. Its frequency and duration are decisive for solar engineering. These are checked

4

through continual measurements, from which the average values are calculated.

In the centre of Switzerland (about 400 m above sea level) the highest values of direct radiation occur at the beginning of April and the end of September. In the area of Zurich (48°N, 400 m altitude) for example, the direct radiation on a sunny day in April at mid-day amounts to $875 W/m^2$ and on 21st December, $775 W/m^2$. In England the values are $700 W/m^2$ and $200 W/m^2$.

Figure 2.1
Spectral irradiance
curves. Solar Energy —
A U.K. assessment (May
1976) (Reproduced
by permission of
UK-ISES)

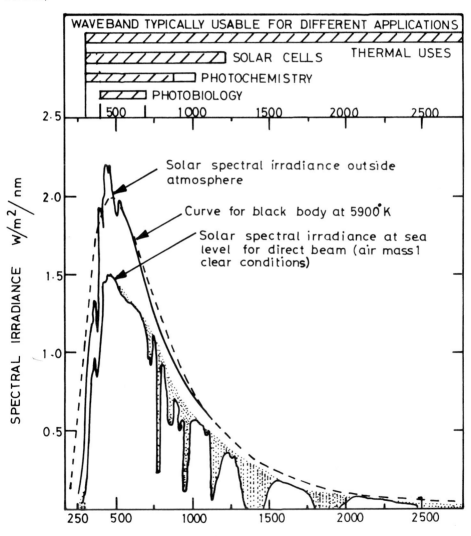

2.2 Diffuse radiation

Diffuse radiation occurs because, in passing through the atmosphere, part of the direct radiation is scattered by floating particles.

The diffuse radiation is distributed differently over the whole hemisphere and is in any case weaker than the direct radiation. It can nevertheless be used for heating. Even in a cloudy winter's day in Central Europe gives an output of 50 300 W/m^2.

Diffuse radiation has no definite orientation, it comes from all directions.

2.3 Total radiation (all-round radiation)

The total radiation is the sum of the direct and the diffuse radiation. It amounts to one of the most important values out of meteorological observation, as it is immediately used for the energy-balance calculation. In London (Lat 52°N) results show a maximum mean monthly daily value of total irradiation for a horizontal surface of 18 MJ/m^2/day (5 kWh/m^2/day) in June and a corresponding minimum of 1.5 MJ/m^2/day (0.42 kWh/m^2/day) in December.

The total irradiation depends upon the orientation of the collecting surface relative to the incoming solar radiation. For example, in Europe in June a horizontal surface receives about twice as much as a vertical surface, i.e. 18 MJ/m^2/day against 10 MJ/m^2/day, but in December less than half as much, i.e. for the horizontal 1.5 MJ/m^2/day against 3.5 MJ/m^2/day for the vertical surface.

From the meteorological data for a particular region, the optimum orientation of a building can be determined, and the optimum angle of the solar collectors fixed.

2.4 Sunshine duration

This is dependent on the geographical position and the climatic conditions. The maximum values are reached in desert areas (e.g. 4000 hours/year in the Sahara) or on high mountains.

The intensity of the radiation and the annual duration of sunshine determine the amount of energy available in a particular geographical situation.

2.5 Radiation intensity

This value given in W/m^2 or kcal/m^2/unit time. At the outer limit of the atmosphere the solar radiation intensity is 1394 W/m^2 (1200 kcal/m^2/hour). At the earth's surface we can reckon in our latitudes with an average value of 635 W/m^2. In very clear sunshine this value can be between 950 W/m^2 and 1220 W/m^2. The average value is about 1000 W/m^2 (860 kcal/m^2/hour).

Example:
Total radiation intensity in Zürich (47° 30'N, altitude 400 m) on
a surface normal to the radiation.

1st May	1200 hr.	1080 W/m²
21st December	1200 hr.	930 W/m²

Figures 2.2 and 2.3 show total (global) radiation values for the
British Isles as given by UK–ISES.

2.6 The practical meaning of solar energy

Mere figures mean little to the layman. However, if we reckon in
familiar units, e.g. money, they assume understandable magnitudes.

Figure 2.2
Annual mean global
daily irradiation (MJ/m²)
as given by UK-ISES.
(Reproduced by per-
mission of UK-ISES)

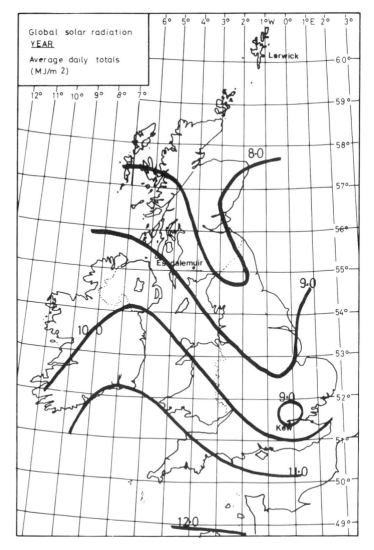

Global solar radiation
YEAR

Average daily totals
(MJ/m 2)

8

Figure 2.3
Monthly mean global irradiation for March, June, September and December,
as given by UK-ISES. (Reproduced by permission of UK-ISES)

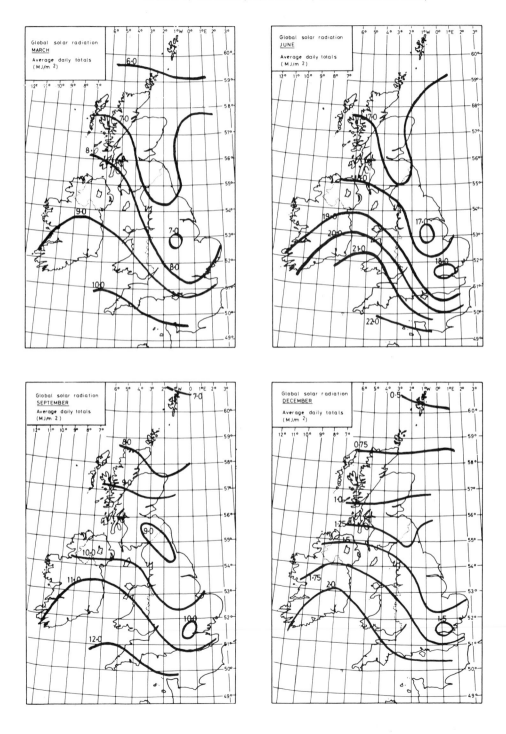

Let us consider a city in the UK which has a clean air legislation, for example, London. How much money's worth of energy does the sun throw on the 100 m² roof of Mr. X, a typical householder? London receives on an average through the year 900 kWh/m² and for a collector efficiency of 45 %, the 100 m² roof would provide 40 500 kWh/year. For electricity at 2p per kWh this represents £805; a gift of £67 per month. What a pity it is that we are not yet in a position to collect this 'money' to good effect. Again, what can the sun mean to a whole country, such as the UK? Although energy consumed in the UK increased to 10.2 GJ $\times$ 10⁹ in 1976, this still only corresponds to the solar energy falling on 1.25 % of the area of the UK.

It can be deduced from these figures that the flow of energy from the sun on to our earth is immeasurably important. Apart from energy, the radiation of the sun possesses many important properties which are already known, and probably some which as yet have remained uninvestigated.

What are the most important natural effects of the sun upon the earth? It is difficult to choose the most important, as it could be said that everything comes from the sun. For example, our relatively warm climate compared to the cold of space, the wind, the movement of billions of tons of water in the form of rain, the photosynthesis of plants, the ocean currents and many more besides.

What technical use can we make of the sun's energy? The possibilities are different for warm and cold climatic conditions. Up to the 40th degree of latitude large and fairly regular amounts of heat are available. In these regions the use of solar energy is already widespread. In Japan for example, several million hot water systems heated by the sun are in operation. Also in Australia, Florida and Israel such installations are in widespread use.

In northern latitudes — between 45° and 55°N — it has been proved that such installations are possible and economical. In Wallasey, near Liverpool (53°N) a school has been heated by solar energy since 1960 (see sub section 9.2). France has had sun heated houses for many years, one being in Chauvency-le-Château, about 49°N (see sub section 9.3). In Switzerland there are examples in Grenchen, Kloten, Bern and other places. In Zürich a yearly average of 1693 hours of sunshine is registered. This provides a yearly free supply of energy of 1160 kWh with an average power of 655 W/m² for each square metre of horizontal surface. The possibilities for use are very varied. In hot countries, where there is often a lot of sun and little water available, sun-powered distillation plants are built for the desalination of sea water (an example is in Bari in Southern Italy).

In desert regions sun-powered machines are in use as water pumps (such as Chinguetti in Mauretania). For research purposes there are sun operated furnaces, which can produce temperatures up to 4000°C (i.e. Odeillo in Southern France).

Electrical energy can also be produced from the sun, but this method is still uneconomic because of the high cost of

Table 2.1   Annual sunshine duration (hours/year)

Berlin	1705	Naples	2396
Berne	1756	New York	2677
Boston	2615	Nice	2775
Brindisi	2591	Paris	1840
Chicago	2611	Perpignan	2560
Copenhagen	1680	Perth	3000
Geneva	1037	Rome	2491
Genoa	2288	Sahara	4000
Graz	1903	Salzburg	1712
Hamburg	1559	Stuttgart	1702
Honalulu	3041	Sydney	3000
Innsbruck	1765	Tel-Aviv	3500
London	1650	Toronto	2045
Los Angeles	3284	Tunis	3200
Lugano	2100	Vancouver	1900
Marseilles	2654	Vienna	1891
Milan	1906	Washington	1540
Munich	1730	Zurich	1694

Table 2.2 Average value of daily hours of sunshine

Month	1	2	3	4	5	6	7	8	9	10	11	12
Aberdeen	2	3	3	5	5	6	5	5	4	3	2	1
Berlin	2	3	5	6	8	8	8	7	6	4	2	1
Birmingham	1	2	3	4	5	6	5	5	4	3	2	1
Boston	5	6	7	7	8	9	10	9	8	6	5	5
Chicago	4	5	6	7	9	10	11	10	8	7	4	4
Hamburg	2	2	4	6	8	8	7	6	6	3	2	1
Honolulu	7	6	8	8	9	9	10	10	9	8	7	7
London (Kew)	2	2	3	5	6	7	6	6	5	3	2	1
Los Angeles	7	7	9	8	9	10	11	11	10	9	8	7
New York	5	6	7	8	9	9	10	9	8	7	6	5
Perth	10	10	8	7	7	6	6	6	9	9	9	10
Sydney	7	7	7	7	7	7	6	6	6	6	6	6
Toronto	3	4	5	6	7	8	9	8	6	5	2	2
Vancouver	2	3	4	6	8	8	10	8	6	4	2	1
Vienna	2	3	4	6	7	8	8	8	7	5	2	1
Washington	4	5	6	7	8	9	10	9	8	7	5	4
Zurich	2	3	5	6	7	7	7	7	6	3	2	2

Table 2.3   Average duration of sunshine for the shortest and longest days

N. Latitude	22 December	22 June	Difference
47°	8 h 26 m	15 h 50 m	7 h 24 m
48°	8 h 18 m	15 h 59 m	7 h 41 m
49°	8 h 9 m	16 h 8 m	7 h 59 m
50°	8 h 0 m	16 h 18 m	8 h 18 m
51°	7 h 50 m	16 h 29 m	8 h 39 m
52°	7 h 40 m	16 h 40 m	9 h 0 m
53°	7 h 29 m	16 h 52 m	9 h 23 m

(From 'Meyers Handbook on the Universe)

Table 2.4   Average possible duration sunshine in hours

Month	47°	48°	49°	50°	51°	52°	53°
January	276	273	269	265	261	256	251
February	286	284	282	280	273	275	273
March	367	366	366	366	366	365	365
April	406	407	409	411	412	414	416
May	464	468	471	475	479	483	488
June	473	477	482	486	491	497	503
July	478	482	486	491	495	500	505
August	439	441	444	447	449	452	455
September	376	377	378	378	379	379	380
October	337	335	334	333	331	330	328
November	281	277	274	271	268	264	260
December	264	260	257	251	246	241	235

Table 2.5   Average yearly radiation totals of all-round radiation (in kWh/m² /year)

Berlin	1000	Marseilles	1860
Boston	1274	Montana	1300
Chigaco	1155	New York	1270
East Sahara	2550	Paris	1500
Florida	1800	Salzburg	1086
Graz	1198	Toronto	1376
Hamburg	930	Vancouver	1270
Honolulu	1883	Vienna	1120
London	927	Washington	1507
Los Angeles	1960	Wurzburg	1081
Lugano	1500	Zurich	1160

Table 2.6

Average hourly values of total radiation in kcal/m²/h south-facing, as a function of time of day and season, measured in 50 % of cases in Kloten (Zurich) between 1963 and 1972.
(P. Valko. Basic information for the use of solar energy. SSES Symposium, Rüschlikon 1974). Some values for London are shown in parenthesis, from U.K. section, International Solar Energy Society).

Hour	Jan	Feb	March	April	May	June	July	Aug	Sept	Oct	Nov	Dec
04-05	0	0	0 (0)	0	15	25 (12)	24	11	0 (0)	0	0	0 (0)
05-06	0	0	11 (0.85)	24	35	46 (53)	47	26	14 (3.4)	0	0	0 (0)
06-07	0	11	30 (11)	46	57	67 (125)	75	51	38 (22)	18	11	0 (0)
07-08	9	29	81 (46)	95	86	94 (210)	121	100	97 (72)	65	22	5 (0)
08-09	51	113	162 (107)	174	171	158 (295)	202	197	190 (145)	135	41	32 (8.5)
09-10	120	201	267 (173)	242	260	251 (365)	307	292	294 (220)	193	74	104 (25)
10-11	189	256	350 (227)	315	330	344 (412)	393	374	416 (281)	257	119	160 (53)
11-12	214	266	393 (258)	365	339	381 (440)	433	425	502 (319)	369	147	201 (76)
12-13	248	313	419 (266)	351	369	404 (444)	442	437	532 (326)	445	167	202 (80)
13-14	214	333	380 (251)	327	362	343 (424)	408	395	490 (310)	434	151	186 (59)
14-15	148	255	301 (214)	262	294	273 (391)	338	338	392 (273)	337	128	123 (55)
15-16	64	135	194 (162)	187	191	180 (339)	232	234	273 (214)	196	64	53 (21)
16-17	10	31	96 (100)	112	120	112 (269)	132	138	142 (147)	65	21	5 (1)
17-18	0	10	31 (41)	50	65	73 (196)	87	62	43 (72)	18	0	0 (0)
18-19	0	0	11 (7)	25	37	53 (124)	57	28	13 (17)	0	0	0 (0)
19-20	0	0	0 (0)	0	17	27 (0)	22	13	0 (0)	0	0	0 (0)

production. Many types of instrument have already been developed (e.g. sun boilers, radios, telephones, clocks) which can be activated with solar energy.

Also in mid-Europe solar energy can be used in the all important role of room and water heating. About 50 % of all energy is used for these purposes and if we only took part of this from the sun we would save several million tons of oil each year.

We are aware of the disadvantages of solar energy — irregular availability, greatly dispersed amounts of energy which make necessary relatively large absorption surfaces, and lastly the problem of storage. On the other hand however, the list of advantages is much greater: pollution free clean energy; collectors can be installed everywhere without any distribution system; energy is available pratically everywhere.

It seems that these advantages are becoming recognised worldwide. Throughout the world researchers, politicians and business people are making use of the great possibilities which solar energy offers us.

Table 2.7   Average value of total radiation in kWh/m^2/day, showing the effect of Latitude.

From W. Diamant 'Techniques and Architecture' September/October 1974 (Transmission coefficient 0.7)

Month	0°	10°	20°	30°	40°	50°	60°	70°	80°	90°
January	5.8	4.8	3.7	2.5	1.3	0.5	0			
February	6.1	5.3	4.3	3.2	2.0	1.0	0.2	0		
March	6.4	6.0	5.3	4.4	3.4	2.2	1.1	0.3	0	
April	6.3	6.3	6.1	5.6	4.9	3.9	2.8	1.7	0.6	0.1
May	5.9	6.3	6.5	6.4	6.1	5.5	4.6	3.6	2.9	2.3
June	5.5	6.2	6.6	6.8	6.7	6.4	5.9	5.2	4.7	4.7
July	5.4	6.1	6.6	6.8	6.8	6.3	6.0	5.3	5.0	4.9
August	5.7	6.2	6.3	6.5	6.2	5.7	5.0	4.0	3.2	3.0
September	6.1	6.3	6.2	5.8	5.1	4.3	3.2	2.1	1.0	0.4
October	6.3	6.0	5.5	4.7	3.7	2.6	1.5	0.5	0	
November	6.1	5.4	4.5	3.5	2.3	1.2	0.4	0		
December	5.8	4.9	3.8	2.6	1.5	0.5	0			
Average value *KWh/m^2/day*	5.95	5.8	5.5	4.9	3.9	3.3	2.5	2.3	2.15	2.5

3 The History of Research into Solar Energy

The sun created the biological basis for human existence, and sun worship was probably the very first religion. Along with other ancient cultures it was the basis of ancient Egyptian belief. In Egypt the sun god Amon Ra was the Sovereign of the Land and the Pharoah was a son of the sun, and enjoyed as such the highest esteem. In India the sun god was called Savitr, the 'Giver of Life', as he awakened the Universe to a new life every morning. The sun god of the Greeks was Helios. He was the image of brightness, warmth, the living-force and fertility. The city of Heliopolis bore his name.

The religion of the ancient Incas has sun worship as its basic symbol. The chiefs of the Incas traced their origin back to the sun god, and the people paid them homage. The sun god also plays an important part in Japan and in the mythologies of many other lands.

In many parts of the earth, temples were built for the worship of the sun; some still exist today, for example, Gizeh, Teotihuacan, Rhodos etc. Socrates (469–399 BC) conceived the idea of a 'Solar House' when he developed a functional house out of the 'Megaron type', which made maximum use of the winter sun, and completely shut out the direct radiation on the South side in summer (see Figure 3.2).

3.1 The start of solar engineering

The first solar engineering advice for architects was given by the Greek historian Xenophon (430–354 BC)

> 'We should build the south side of the houses higher to catch the winter sun.'

The first knowledge of solar energy technique came from the Greek mathematician Euclid (about 300 BC), who worked in the Plato Academy in Alexandria; in his work he described the theory of spherical reflectors. But the greatest of the ancient solar engineers was Archimedes (287–212 BC), whose researches into

14

Figure 3.1
The concave mirror of
Archimedes

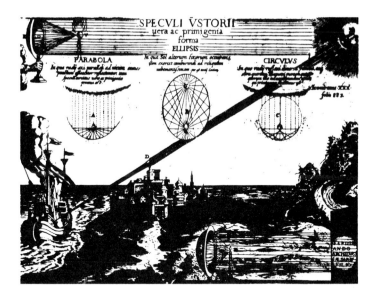

Figure 3.2
The 'Solar House Con-
ception' of Socrates
1. Solar radiation on the
South face in summer
2. Solar radiation on the
South face in winter
3. Covered terrace
4. Living room
5. Store room as ther-
mal buffer zone
6. Insulating wall to the
North

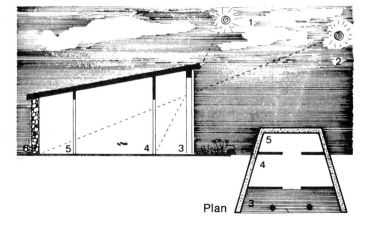

Figure 3.3
The 'Burning Glass' of
Bernieres and Trudaine
1774

solar energy produced not only theoretical, but also important practical results. By means of concave mirrors, whose focus, as a result of very small curvatures, was several hundred metres distant, he was able to set on fire the ships of the Roman general Marcus Claudius Marcellus during the two year siege of the Sicilian capital Syracuse. In the same way Proclus in the year 514 AD is supposed to have destroyed a fleet of the Goths at Constantinople.

The possibility of this technical achievement has since been proved many times (e.g. J. L. Buffon set fire to a pile of wood at a distance of 60 m). Heron of Alexandria (about 100 AD) also produced 'burning mirrors' and after Plutarch (about 50–125 AD) there was a burning mirror which kindled the sacred flame of the temple of Vesta in ancient Rome.

The Arabs already possessed the knowledge that ordinary glass had the property of concentrating the heat of the sun, and after the conquest of Egypt they learnt the manufacture of glass which was flourishing there, and soon made glass vessels (retorts) for the distillation of liquids by solar radiation. Primitive burning glasses were even found in the ruins of Niniva in Mesopotania. In Europe the problem of solar heat only became interesting again after the invention of the lens by Galilei (1564–1642). In 1615 the French engineer Salomon de Caus (1576–1626) described in his script 'Raison des forces mouvantes' a water lifting machine operated by the sun's heat, which he called a 'perpetual fountain'.

Many other scientists* built various machines and other devices operating with solar energy by means of lenses and mirrors.

The Swiss physicist de Saussure (1740–1799) from Geneva built the first modern storage system for the heat from the sun. He arranged five sheets of glass so that, at any given time, two layers of glass were separated by an air space. The air between the layers of glass substantially increased the heating effect, and de Saussure achieved by this means a temperature of up to 87.5°C. Modern surface collectors work on this principle. In 1872 a 'Sun-distiller' installation was built in a desert in N. Chile which produced 27 000 litres of drinking water a day from salt water. But the 19th century was mainly the century of the sun power machine. The first modern machine goes back to the Frenchman August Bernard Mouchot. On 22nd September 1864 near Algiers he set his installation in motion. This great machine had a mirror of 5 m diameter, and the water pump provided 2.5 tons of water per minute.

---

*Y. B. Porta, Drebbel, R. Fludd, A. Martina, A. Kircher, Milliet Dechales, Bernard de Belidor, Walter von Tschirhaus, L. Buffon, D. Trudaine, A. Lavoisier, Joseph Priestly, M. Bernieres, Mariotte, Dufay, Ducaria, Herschel, Melloni, Pouillet, Magini, de Flaugergues, Laprovostaye, Desains, Magini, Villette, Hoesen, Ducarla, De la Cliche, Oliver Evans, Deliancurt, Cagniard-Latour, Laubereau, Frot and others.

In 1878, at the Paris World Exhibition, Professor Mouchot presented another sun machine which drove a newspaper printing press (see Figure 3.4). He also published the first modern book on solar energy 'Solar Heat and its Industrial Applications'. At about the same time the American John Ericson (1803–1889)

Figure 3.4
Sun power machine by A. Mouchot (1878). From the book by J. Payen 'Histoires des sources d'energie' (History of sources of energy)

Figure 3.5
Sun collector by T. F. Nichols (about 1908). From the book by O. Kausch 'The immediate Use of Solar Energy'

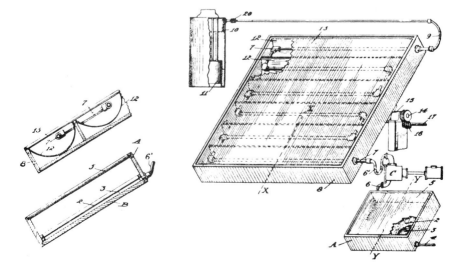

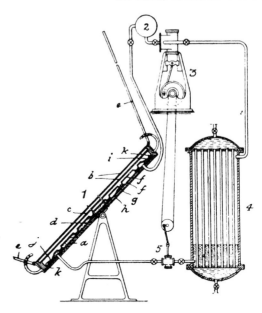

built a small 2.5 h.p. sun machine, and worked for ten years from 1870–1880 on a sunpower-station, which unfortunately was never built.

3.2 Progress in the early 1900s

From 1902 to 1908 H. E. Willsie and John Boyle in California built sun machines of 6 h.p. and 20 h.p. In 1901, A. G. Aneas built a machine of 15 h.p. and in the same year the famous solar steam installation of Pasadena was made. In 1911, Frank Shuman and C. V. Boys in Philadelphia completed a model sun powered installation, which, two years later, was put into operation in Meadi, Egypt, 16 km from Cairo. This 100 h.p, machine served for irrigation purposes, and provided a 4200 m² cotton plantation with water pumped out of the Nile.

In 1921 Professor Dr. Rudolf Straubel of Zeiss in Jena made a sun furnace which brought an iron bar to melting point in a few seconds.

After 1918 in the USA a large number of solar energy patents were filed, and several of these devices were put into operation. In those days, the most notable man in this field was C. G. Abbott. Apart from various other apparatus he built solar hot water plants, which were put into production a few years later, and made possible large savings in energy in the Southern States.

The first large sun powered installation for research purposes was produced in Tashkent (Soviet Union) in 1933. At the same time an installation was proposed, which was supposed to have provided enough energy for a whole city, but which was never put into operation.

The first experiments in using solar energy directly for domestic purposes were made between 1920 and 1940. Alexander McNeilledge in California constructed a building with surface sun collectors for hot water and space heating. (Scotty's Castle in Death Valley 1922–29).

In 1931 the German architect Martin Wagner introduced his project for the competition 'The Growing House'. A glass skin protected the outer walls from the effects of the weather, and provided a space which reduced the loss of heat, and utilised the incoming solar radiation.

Most of the solar houses of those years (e.g. G. F. Keck, Illinois Institute of Technology 1940; F. W. Hutchinson Purdue, University of Indiana 1945) were only 'solar' in so far as they had large glass panes on the south side.

This single measure was not enough as, in sunshine, the house was too hot, and without sun much too cold. In winter even more fuel was needed than for other houses. The heat storage problem had not been solved.

Between 1930 and 1940 the great significance of the sun for health purposes was again recognised. In the struggle against tuberculosis, buildings with large windows to catch as much sun as possible were built in many places, mainly in the Swiss mountains. All modern architects of the era recognised the sun as the most important influence on house design. In 1939 the first Massachusetts Institute of Technology (MIT) 'Solar House' was produced. The working group was under the leadership of James Hottle and B. Woertz.

Figure 3.7
Solar power station in
Font-Romeu, France

The first large building extensions fitted with solar hot water generators were produced in Florida in 1939 (Edison Court Extensions). The sun collectors were of steel with double glazing, and the flat oval shaped tubes were of copper. The water was heated to 83°C in a few hours. The first sun collectors to be put into production were made by the firm Pan American Solar Heater Inc.

3.3 Solar energy developments subsequent to 1945

In California, Florida, Texas and Arizona the use of solar heaters had already been widespread since the 1940's. Telkes—Raymond—Peabody of Dover, Massachusetts (USA) built in 1948 the first solar house, in which 80 % of the heating requirement was provided by solar energy.

Subsequent to 1945 solar energy research received a great uplift because of the beginning of difficulties in energy supply. Almost everywhere in the world scientists and others recognised the great significance of solar energy.[1]

In industry many large and small firms in all parts of the world made important contributions towards research.[2] After 1950 the first large symposia were arranged mainly through various American Universities and Research Institutes.[3] In October 1954 Unesco and the Indian Government organised the first important international conference which was concerned exclusively with solar and wind energy.

In October 1955 in Phoenix, Arizona, the Association for Applied Solar Energy was formed, and at the same time an international Symposium and the first Solar Engineering Exhibition were staged. A thousand scientists from thirty-six countries took part in this event, at which about eighty solar devices were exhibited.

---

[1] *America:* Dr. Maria Telkes, Dr. Georges Löf, Dr. H. C. Hottel, Dr. F. Daniels, H. B. Sargent, Dr. J. Hobsob, D. Farrington, I. Duffie, R. P. Lappala, John Jellott, W. L. Lucking, S. Andrassy, R. N. Morse, R. Krause, R. C. Jordan, J. Ostermeyer, G. Benveniste, W. Rhodes, Dr. S. Laszio, C. J. Kevane, W. M. Conn, P. E. Glaser, M. Kastens.
United Kingdom: Dr. H. Heywood, E. Golding, L. Gardner, E. Curtis.
France: Prof. Felix Trombe, Dr. Touchais, Prof. Perrot, M. Foex.
Israel: Dr. N. Robinson, Dr. H. Tabor, R. Sabotka.
Italy: Prof. Giorgio Nebbia, Prof. G. Gaetano, Dr. V. Storelli, C. Garbato, A. Chierici.
South Africa: Austin Whillier.
Switzerland: J. Sutter, G. Adank, Seehaus, E. Schönholzer, Auguse Piccard.
Russia: F. Molaro, Dr. V. A. Baum.
Spain: Prof. C. Azcarraga, Prof. P. Blanco.
Japan: H. Tamiya, M. Yanagimachi, Seizo Goto, I. Tanishita.
Lebanon: A. Tarcici.
Canada: E. A. Allcut.
India: M. L. Ghai, K. N. Mathur and M. L. Khana were the modern pioneers of the new technology.

In 1956 the first modern journal on solar energy appeared: *The Sun at Work*. One year later, *The Journal of Solar Energy Science and Engineering* was published.

This intensive research work led to many practical results. In America, Russia, Japan and France even larger sun power and smelting furnace installations were built.

In many countries such as Japan, Australia, Israel, Cyprus and South Africa solar water heaters have become commonplace. With increasing frequency one hears of houses which are heated or air conditioned by solar energy.

Between 1945 and 1959 the following important pioneer solar houses were built:

Boulder house in Colorado by G. Löf (1945)
MIT Solar house No. 2 by H. C. Hottel (1947)
Dover house in Massachusetts by Telkas, Raymond, Peabody (1948)
MIT Solar house No. 3 by H. C. Hottel (1949)
State College New-Mexico house by L. Gardenshire (1953)
Lefever Solar house by H. R. Lefever (1954)
Amado, Arizona house by Denovan, Raymond, Bliss (1954)
University of Toronto house by E. A. Allcut (1956)
Solar office buildings in Alburquerque by H. Bridgers and D. Paxton (1956)
Solar house in Tokyo by M. Yanagimachi (1956)
Solar house in Bristol (England) by L. Gardner (1956)
Rickmansworth house by E. Curtis in England (1956)
MIT Solar house No. 4 by H. C. Hottel (1958)
Benedict-Canyon house by R. White (1958)
Solar house in Casablanca by C. M. Shaw & Ass. (1958)
Solar House in Nagoya (Japan) by M. Yanagimachi (1958)
Denver house in Colorado by G. Löf (1959)
Princeton Univ. house by A. Olgyay (1959)
Solar office house in Tucson by R. Bliss (1959)
Thomason Solar house No. 1 by A. Thomason (1959)

---

[2] General Dynamics Corp., Kennecott Copper Corporation, Bell-Telephone-Laboratories Co., Du-Pont, Arthur D. Little Inc., Convair, Curtiss-Wright Corporation, American-Saint Gobain Corp., Lochhead Aircraft, Westinghouse, Northcrop Aircraft, Revere Copper and Brass, Brown Electronic, Shell Development Company, Strong Electric Corp., Admiral Corp., W. M. C. Precision Works, Sandia Corp., Arizona Public Services Co. in America. Radiosol AG in Marocco, Patek Phillip AG (Switzerland), Miromit AG and Sun Heaters Ltd. in Israel, Delta Steel Mill Co. in Egypt, Mizoshiri AG, Goto Optical, Jiro Ono industrie Comp., Sun Thermatics Co., Kyowa Works, Tokuho Shikanai, Takata Aluminium Works, Taisei Sun Heat Co., Senjuro Kaneko, Nippon Electric Co. in Japan and many others.

[3] Massachusetts Institute of Technology, University of Utah, University of Minnesota, Batella Memory Inst. University of California, Ohio Academy of Sciences, University of Wisconsin, Stanford Inst., University of Arizona, University of Florida, Fordham University, Harward University etc.

Already these solar houses belong to architectural history, not on aesthetic grounds, but because subsequently there have been technically interesting innovations which differ from the earlier common methods of construction. An important invention of this early period was the solar cell introduced by Bell Telephone Laboratories in New York in 1954. This device, which converts solar energy directly into electric current, will soon be applicable

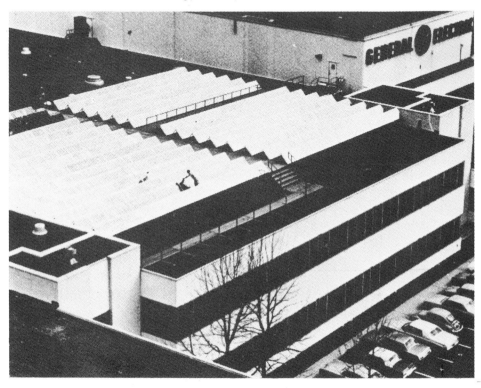

Figure 3.8 (above) GEC canteen with solar panels in the USA

Figure 3.9 (below) American house with direct solar heating (Thomason-Kollektoren)

economically, not only for space flight, but also for domestic purposes. In March 1957 the first solar architecture competition took place in Phoenix (Arizona) under the motto: 'Life with the Sun'. About 1400 architects from many countries of the world participated. Peter R. Lee from Minneapolis won the first prize, his project was built in 1958 (AFASE Solar House Phoenix with L. Gardenshire).

From 1958 because oil was relatively cheap the development of solar energy had substantially slowed down, but had not stopped.

In 1961 UNO held an important conference in Rome under the title 'New Sources of Energy'. Several hundred scientists from about thirty countries took part in about 250 discussion groups on solar, wind and geothermal energy. (UN conference on New Sources of Energy). France, Italy, Israel and New Zealand organised exhibitions in which interesting prototypes from all branches of solar energy application were presented.

In September 1961, the NATO Scientific Council organised a Symposium on solar energy in Greece (the Sounion Seminar). The participants came from Greece, France, India, Israel, Italy, Japan, New Zealand, Portugal, Spain, Turkey, England, USA and West Germany. These conferences eventually produced, both in Europe and elsewhere, the first practical results, mainly in the field of solar room heating.

3.4 European Solar Houses

In 1956 the first European solar houses were built in England by Gardner and Curtis. Paradoxically these buildings were in a country which has relatively little sunshine compared to other parts of Europe. In 1961, the architect A. E. Morgan in Wallasey, near Liverpool, built St. George's School which is heated with solar energy. This building is one of the largest solar buildings in Europe (see Chapters 5 and 9).

The first French solar house was built — at first only for research purposes — in 1962 by the French Research Institute CNRS in Odeillo (Pyrenees) under the leadership of Dr. Trombe. In 1968 the architect J. Michel built two more solar houses in the same region, and in 1972 built a further solar house in Chauvency-le-Chateau in N. E. France. All these solar houses were built to the patented Trombe-Michel-System, in which the air heated by the sun warms the building by natural convection. The collectors are mounted vertically on the south side.

Following the architectural pioneer work of Jaques Michel in France, we should mention another architect from Paris George Alexandroff. In Chinguetti (Mauretania) in a region with water supply difficulties, Alexandroff built an installation in which roof-mounted sun collectors receive enough energy to deliver water for two thousand people with the help of solar pumps (1.5 h.p. Masson-Girardier system). The building is also well integrated architecturally. Elements from the traditional architecture of the region are employed. This example shows what notable results good cooperation between architects and solar engineers can produce.

The Unesco conference in July 1973 in Paris, with the title 'The Sun in the Service of Man' gave fairly exact information on the state of solar energy in the world. Eight hundred scientists from sixty countries took part in this Symposium. Several solar architecture projects were described, such as:

California solar house by H. R. Hay.
Solar One house by K. Böer.
University of Florida solar house by E. Farber.
Terrace dwelling by D. Chanson and P. Claux.
Solar oasis project by G. Alexandroff.

This Unesco conference which took place a few months before the oil crisis, closed a whole era of solar energy research. Up to 1973 the problem of solar energy was a field of research for scientists, but from then on it has become a matter of concern and great significance for the whole world. From what was originally an object of research has come a new industry, which concerns us all — politicians, contractors, architects, builders, house owners. Also the 'man in the street', who perhaps is not directly interested in the building industry or energy economics, but who in the end must pay for any waste of energy, has a vital interest.

4 Economic Policy Aspects of Solar Engineering

It has been seen from the previous chapters, that solar energy engineering is no new science. On the other hand, in the politics of energy supply in various countries it has up to now played a minor part. Indeed, in many places, solar energy was regarded as quite unimportant, and often impossible to use as an energy source.

Nowadays the situation looks quite different. The oil crisis of 1973 and the world wide atom-power controversy have brought the problem of solar energy into the open, so that today it is no longer 'Yes' or 'No' which is disucssed, but 'When' and 'How?'

Hans Matthöfer, Minister of Research and Technology in the Republic of Germany, put this new 'official recognition' of solar energy very much to the point:

'Solar energy acquires increasing meaning in the discussion on energy supply. It is the only technically usable source of energy known at the present time which can supply man with energy for a practically unlimited time and which, in addition, is especially pollution-free. The limited duration of supplies of fossil energy was brought into general awareness by the events of 1973. Since then all over the world the search has increased into the use of other sources of energy. Solar energy takes a central place in these efforts.'

The eminent scientist Wernher von Braun said at the opening of the Unesco Congress:

'The Sun in the service of Man: Man finds himself on the threshold of a new era, which could be called 'The Age of the Sun'.

The new direction in energy politics was given expression in a report in *'Neue Zürcher Zeitung'* on the energy research programme of the USA:

'The Energy Research and Development Administration (ERDA), the organisation succeeding the Atomic Energy Commission, and which has been in existence since the beginning of the year, has submitted to the President and Congress a study on the short, mid and long term

25

execution of the USA energy policy, which should be placed on as diversified a basis as possible . . .'

'The commercial use of the quick breeder reactor, which was originally considered for 1987 is being delayed until the 21st century.'

'In its report ERDA brings solar energy to the same level as the quick breeder and nuclear fusion. These three energy sources are identified as the long term dominants of the energy policy.'

The last two sentences of the report are especially important, as they give the comparison of atomic and solar energy through the Energy Research and Development Administration, which means a basic change in American energy policy. These new priorities of US energy research will soon have a world wide effect, and will force other countries to reconsider energy policy.

What are the practical aspects now — several years after the oil crisis — of solar energy in the domestic field, in economical and political respects in various countries? The following paragraphs illustrate the developments which are taking place.

4.1 USA

The USA which possesses enormous sunny areas, has been at the forefront of solar energy research since the turn of the century, and could maintain this lead. Although the US government is still oriented today towards an atomic priority, it nevertheless gives substantial help in direct and indirect ways towards solar energy research. Even the AEC (Atomic Energy Commission) has its own solar research laboratories.

Most help (from the State) is given through NASA (National Aeronautics and Space Administration), NSF (National Science Foundation) and HUD (Housing and Urban Development). In September 1974, President Ford ratified a law which allowed a special budget for solar space heating purposes (Solar Heating and Cooking Demonstration Act).

The State Budget for solar research amounted to 89 million dollars for 1975. The Senate provided 100 million dollars in 1976. This sum is very large if one realises that, for 1970, the same Budget was practically nil, 1.6 million in 1972, and only 3.8 million in 1973. For the next ten to fifteen years 2 to 3 billion dollars will be made available for solar energy purposes. Private industry is investing even more. About eighty large firms, including giants such as General Electric, Westinghouse, Motorola, Du-Pont, Honeywell, Corning, P.P.G. Industries and Arthur D. Little Inc., are together studying the market possibilities with the help of specialised institutions.

The conclusion is that the solar energy industry for domestic purposes (room heating, hot water and cooking systems) can mean a market of 1.3 billion dollars by 1985. According to

Arthur D. Little Inc. this situation would in fifteen years make the USA completely independent of other countries for energy. The investments of these firms are probably in proportion to the expected profits, but detailed figures are not available. Solar hot water storage systems which during and after the Second World War were already widely used in the Southern States have again become popular.

Several firms such as Daylin Inc., Tranter Inc., Burke Rubber Co., Fun and Frolic, Helio Assoc. Inc., Revere Copper and Brass, P.P.G. Industries, Motorola Inc., Meinel Helio Assoc Inc., produce installations which for 'Do-it-yourself' applications can be had already for 100 dollars. According to manufacturers' statements it is possible to buy a swimming bath heating system for 18.95 dollars. In the USA more than 1.3 million swimming pools are already heated from the sun.

For space heating purposes, solar installations are already offered for 100 to 200 dollars. Complete solar space heating systems are also on the market for prices such as 107 dollars per square metre of collector surface, and sun collectors alone for 62 dollars per square metre.

The number of sun heated buildings in the USA amounts to several hundred, and includes several large structures such as:

Grover Cleveland Junior High School in Dorchester, Mass;
Timonium Elementary School in Maryland;
North View Junior High School in Minneapolis, Minn;
Fauquier High School in Warrenton, Virginia.

Figure 4.1
Fauquier high school,
Warrenton
Virginia, USA

In a study in 1972, carried out by the authors R. Cherry and R. Morse for the US Solar Energy Authority (Conclusions and Recommendations of the United States Solar Energy Panel) it was claimed that with the necessary support of research, solar energy can, in the next decades, provide 35 % of the energy requirements for the air conditioning of buildings in the USA. (Also 10 % of the liquid fuel and 20 % of the electric power requirements up to the year 2020 could be supplied by solar energy.) In order to further this progress, some American States, such as Indiana, give tax advantages to house owners who fit their buildings with solar heating. The long term outlook for solar energy on the USA is given by *'Neue Zürcher Zeitung'*:

'In one of the reports on the American energy policy, which the Energy Research and Development Administration published in mid-1975, the outlook and possibilities of solar energy in the next half century are made clear. In the overall energy policy plan published at the end of June, the ERDA had attempted to examine the options of the United States, and to develop a long-term strategy, which should guarantee the country among others the corresponding political independence and economic power. In this strategy, solar energy, together with nuclear fusion and the quick breeder, was identified as one of the main long term sources of energy.

According to the strategy represented by the ERDA, the sun, hardly used up to now as an energy supply, should provide about a quarter of the USA energy requirements up to the year 2020, and should be able to contribute to the reduction of imports of oil — all the more so as by that time the American production of oil and natural gas should have been allowed to become insignificant.

To broaden the role of solar energy a three-part effort is necessary. Firstly — and this represents in the shorter view, the one promising most success — its direct use for heating and cooling purposes will be aimed at the private as well as the industrial and agricultural spheres. Secondly, solar energy should be able to be converted into electricity, whereby an inexhaustible source of electricity would be won; this aim has, in the long term, the highest priority. Thirdly, solar energy should be used for obtaining gas from manure, wood and other agricultural waste; this technique, known as biological will, as represented in the report, certainly not be able to make an appreciable contribution to energy conservation until the next century.

In order to make solar energy practicable for these purposes, says the report, costs must be considerably reduced. According to the ERDA statement a heating and cooling installation in a one family house, based on solar energy, costs between 3000 and 8000 dollars. Conversion of existing houses to solar energy costs four times as much. With a five year demonstration programme supported by the Government, a 30 % to 40 % cost reduction can be achieved. In the present fiscal year 89 million dollars will be applied to solar energy research. In comparison, the budget four years ago amounted to 1 million dollars.'

4.2 Japan

Since mythological times the Japanese have recognised the significance of the sun. Today Japan and the USA stand together in the forefront in the use of solar energy.

In the Solar Exhibition in Tokyo in 1956 about fifteen firms exhibited solar water heaters. Today about 3.5 million such installations are in operation in Japan. At Keio University an installation with 66 m^2 in Japan of sun collector surface is in operation. The first Japanese solar house was built by Yanagimachi in 1956, and two others in 1960 in Tokyo and Funabasha City, also by the same constructor. The following firms are some of those who are engaged on producing solar building devices:

Goto Optical MFG Co.
Hitachi Chemical Co. Ltd.
Sekisui Chemical Co. Ltd.
Shizuoka Seiki Co. Ltd.
Matsushia Electric Works Ltd.
Marno Sangyo Kaisha Ltd.

The most important research centre is the State Solar Research Laboratory in Nagoya. At the beginning of 1975, Japan started a 'Sunshine Programme' the aims of which reach into the year 2000. The government wishes to establish several sun-power stations in mountainous areas of central Japan. Other installations are planned near already existing atom powered plants. For the first year of research the equivalent of about £6.7 million were made available from the State Budget.

4.3. Australia

The Australian Ministry of Science has also introduced a solar energy utilisation programme. The research work is continuing under the 'Commonwealth Scientific and Industrial Research Organisation' which is supported by the Government.

The Australian Department of Housing and Construction has set up a programme whereby sun collectors of 3–4 m^2 and storage tanks of 180–360 litres will be installed in all public buildings. It is calculated that by utilising solar energy for water heating, it is possible to provide in this way at least 65 % of the total hot water requirements. In several hotels and colleges high output solar water heaters are in operation, e.g. Don Hotel in Darwin (30 m^2 sun collectors with a 950 litre storage tank); Ross Smith Hotel in Darwin (24 m^2 collectors with 2275 litre storage tank) and Sacred College in Adelaide (60 m^2 collectors with storage tanks of 4100 litre total capacity).

Solar water heaters are widely used, and 3000–4000 new installations are produced annually, also for export. Several solar houses have already been completed or are under construction.

The financial expenditure up to the year 2000 is estimated to be about £4.5 million.

4.4 United Kingdom

The first European solar houses were built in the UK. These were the Rickmansworth house near London by E. Curtis in 1956 and the solar house in Bristol by L. Gardner in 1956. Experts in the UK, which on a cloudy February day still has 60 W/m^2 diffuse radiation, are convinced that this energy can still be used. In 1974 the Anglesey house (S. V. Szokolay) was built and, in 1974, the Milton Keynes Development Corporation (MKDC) also produced a solar house with 40 m^2 sun collectors (S. V. Szokolay, P. Atherton and D. Hodges). It is now possible to build the Cambridge Autonomous House, based on theoretical studies begun in 1971, in which the total energy requirements (heating, cooling and electric power) will be provided by solar and wind energy (Project by A. Pike, J. Thring, G. Smith and J. Littler), see sub section 9.9.

Royston Summers are planning twenty-nine solar heated flats, and Dominic Michaelis has several solar house projects under study. Many firms are making solar collectors, and several larger institutes are carring out research work.

The Times of 5th May 1977 reported a Department of Energy statement that: 'By the year 2000 Britain should be getting 8% of her energy from renewable sources such as the sun and waves. The Government was now spending nearly £10 m a year on research into renewable sources of energy. This includes £ 6.4 m on solar energy, £2.3 m on wave energy and £0.8 m on geothermal energy sources.'

4.5 France

The French research programme for solar architecture is proceeding under the leadership of State Institutes such as CNRS

(Centre Nationale de la Recherche Scientifique), ANVAR (Agence Nationale de Valorisation de la Recherche), EDF (Electricité de France), University of Marseilles and others.

In 1973, 1974 and 1975 several solar houses by the architect J. Michel were presented at the 'Foire de Paris' Exhibition. In Aramon, near Nimes, and in Le Havre, six solar houses are under construction (J. Michel and G. Alexandroff) with the help of the above mentioned Institutes. Other architects such as D. Chanson, P. Claux and Guy Rottier (Ecopolis Project) are working on various solar projects.

Several firms such as Sofée, Sarl, Caillol SA, Paturle, Diemo, Cerca, Sofretes, Situb, St. Gibain, Cegedur-Pechiney, St. Helio Système, Ste. Helibat, R.T.C. are carrying out important pioneer work and are already producing solar engineering components in quantity.

There are also tax advantages for the installation of solar equipment in order to further technical progress in the use of solar energy. The French New Energy Sources Research and Development Programme 1975 had a budget equivalent to £8.37 million.

4.6 Germany

In 1975 Herr Matthofer, the West German minister responsible for energy, explained to the Press in Bonn:

'The economic use of solar energy for the provision of heat is also possible in West Germany with recoverable expenditure. In the short term it will be possible to obtain a significant part of hot water supplies in the summer with the help of solar energy. Today, in the summer, hot water is often produced with very low efficiency in oil heating installations. In the longer term, the use of solar energy for space heating purposes can also be considered.'

In this connection Herr Matthofer introduced two definite advancement projects by his ministry. An experimental house of the Philips Research Laboratories Aachen, as well as a swimming bath in Wiehl heated with solar energy (Oberbergischer Kreis).

The solar house in Aachen is being produced by the Philips Research Laboratory and the Rheinisch-Westfälischen Elecktri-zätswerken (RWE), State financing being 50%. The insulation is five times better than that of traditional houses and should provide almost the whole heating requirements with the $20m^2$ sun collectors. The house is being used as a demonstration for architects and heating specialists, to further the spread of this new technique. Computers will simulate the use of the house by a family for about two years before a family takes over for further studies.

The solar heated swimming bath at Wiehl was built by the firm Brown Boveri, Mannheim (Figures 4.2 and 4.3). In this case 1500 m² of collectors heat the water. Brown Boveri carried out measurements with solar-thermal collectors in 1974, which show that in spite of the bad weather conditions, from May to September about 2.5 kWh/m²/day of energy in the form of heat could be obtained with one of the collectors developed in West Germany. The collectors consist of individual sections which could be reasonably produced in a workshop. Based on these results, plans were evolved for producing and installing these collectors on a larger scale.

Thus, on the one hand, the collectors should be subjected to long term tests, on the other hand, the possibility of the use of solar energy should be demonstrated by publicising specific demonstrations. Further, the manufacturing techniques in the industry should be tried and proved in a pre-production programme. At the same time exact cost estimates become possible, which are an essential prerequisite for an introduction to the market.

The use of solar energy is particularly convenient for the auxiliary heating of open air baths, because the necessary water temperatures (about 26°C, on colder days up to 28°C) are low in comparison to the hot water used in the home. According to the press announcement of 1975, West Germany has other important solar energy projects in view. One of these concerns a proposition made by the Schleswig Holsteiner Landgesellschaft mbH, of Kiel, to instal a solar heating plant as a demonstration installation, in a garden city (20 businesses) in Gönnebeck, Kreis

Figure 4.2
Solar heated swimming bath in Wiehl (Germany)

Segeberg. This would be used for the heating of a market hall, and for the cultivation area of a greenhouse yet to be drawn up. The total cost is estimated to be about 4 million DM. Other current works proposed are:

Water heating with solar energy (BBC and RWE).

Special solar absorption surfaces for obtaining heat. (Dornier, further development of the absorber developed for the desalination plant).

Modular sun house heating and cooling system (Messerschmitt, Bölkow and Blohm).

Development of high temperature stable solar absorption surfaces (Dornier).

Study of non-fossil and non-nuclear energy sources for the future supply of energy (AGF).

Study of long term heat storage (MBB).

Experimental study of the development of terrestrial solar-cell generators (AEG).

Figure 4.3
The installation in the Wiehl pilot scheme is the solar energy collector for heating water in the swimming-bath. The collector is on the surface of the roof (1500m²) of the Wiehl leisure centre. During October to May the pool is used as an ice-rink. In the coldest months November to March (approx) the energy taken from the ice rink heat-pumps is used to heat the hall.

A solar research laboratory is operating in Stuttgart under the leadership of Dr Werner Bloss. The Nikolaus Laing Research Institute in Aldingen near Stuttgart is also working on solar projects, including the Energy-Cascade-Project. This Institute wants to bring solar energy obtained in Spain, North Africa and Southern Italy to central Europe in the form of hot water.

International cooperation with the Western partner States, in particular with the USA is defined by West German energy minister Herr Matthöfer as 'very close'. For 1975, he announced the signing of a multilateral cooperation agreement for the exploration of solar energy under the secretaryship of the USA. In 1975, the Ministry of Research and Technology made available about 21.5 million DM (£5 million) for research work on solar energy in space) and up to 1979 about 110 million DM (£26 million). Today there are already some hundreds of houses having solar heating in operation.

4.7 Soviet Union

After America and Japan the Soviet Union is the third country in the world where the harnessing of solar energy has made the most progress. The first important solar engineering installations were built in the 1930's.

In America the chief applications of solar energy are for swimming pool heating and in Japan, hot water installations. The Soviet Union, which has about 1 million square kilometres of uninhabited land reserves, is mainly interested in the wider use of solar pumps and stills. There are many regions where the duration of sunshine reaches very high values (about 3000 hours per year in Central Asia) and the economic use of various solar installations is especially advantageous. Solar research plants are spread over the whole country and coordination is achieved through the Krijanovsky Energy Institute in Moscow.

Several large projects are under construction, such as the solar furnace of Jerevan, where each 10 m diameter parabolic collector produces 50 kW of electrical power, and can thus supply various types of solar equipment (hot water installations, refrigerators, solar stills, cookers, etc) for domestic purposes. A quantity of solar equipment of various types has already been produced industrially in relatively large numbers (25 000 units in 1974).

From information received from Unesco, it would seem that Russian scientists are quite sure that the twenty-first century will be when solar energy comes into its own.

4.8 Switzerland

In June 1974 the 'Schweizercsche Vereinigung für Sonnenergie' (SSES) (Swiss Association for Solar Energy) was formed in

Berne. It has over one thousand members from industry, the professions, science and the private sector. Rene Schärer of Grenchen, Bruno Schneider of Kloten and J. P. Winkler of Bern have produced solar heating systems for water and space heating. In 1975 the Association drew up a National Oil-saving Plan which was laid before the National, Local and State governing bodies. The SSES proposes that all the houses in Switzerland be provided with solar collectors (1.2 m^2 for each house owner) which would thereby save about 1 million tons of oil per year.

Switzerland's first solar-heated factory-office building will soon be in operation. This is the 'Micafil-Project by P. R. Sabady (see sub-section 9.11). Several solar projects are being studied, such as the Delta Stadt (Delta City) project near Bern (by G. Wirth, Arch.ETH/SIA and Dr. T. P. Woodmann ETH); the 'Plenar-Project' (by the Plenar Group) and others.

4.9. Other countries

Solar architecture projects are also being carried out in countries such as Sweden (solar house in the University town of Lund by C. H. Olsen), Holland (solar house in Oss by Elemans and Van Koppen), Denmark (Zero Energy House by Korsgaard, Harboe, Kjerule-Jensen), Italy (Swedish solar house in Capri by G. Pleijel and B. Lindstrom, and Project Sun City by G. Francia.

In Greece, Turkey, Israel, Cyprus, Iraq, India, Morocco, Spain, Portugal, Chile, Iran, Mexico, Venezuela and Argentine solar hot water systems are in use. In many countries these systems already have the same importance as all other aspects of the building industry.

In 1973, the NATO Committee for 'The Challenges of Modern Sciences' (CCMS) approved a research programme for the use of solar energy and made available about £1 million for research purposes. In 1973 the CCMS undertook a Community Project for the harnessing of solar energy in Brussels. Japan and Sweden, who do not belong to NATO, also joined this important international activity.

The EEC (European Economic Community) has a provisional programme for solar energy research and development under active review, which budgets for an average of around £2 million per annum for the next four years.

5 Solar Energy for Domestic Purposes

The sun irradiates all regions of our earth with energy. The amount of this energy received annually is dependent on the geographical and climatic conditions, but we can say that the practical use of this energy is possible everywhere in the world. Naturally on the Red Sea where the sun shines about 4000 hours every year, it is easier and cheaper to benefit from it than in Scandinavia, where there are only 1200 hours of sun (per year) and also at a lower intensity.

The most important possible uses of solar energy for domestic purposes are:

The production of hot water.
Room heating.
Room cooling and air-conditioning.
Swimming pool heating.

5.1 Solar hot water systems

When the rays of the sun fall on any surface, its temperature rises above that of the surrounding air. This rise in temperature is the result of the development of heat in this surface through absorption of the sun's radiant energy. If we form an enclosure under this surface, and let water circulate in it, the water will be heated as a result. How quickly an amount of water reaches a certain temperature is dependent on how many useful calories the sun gives us and how the absorption elements (sun collectors) and the storage elements (tanks/boilers) are engineered (efficiency, heat losses, etc.).

Dr. C. G. Abbott who is one of the greatest pioneers of solar energy research describes in his book *'How one uses the heat of the Sun'* a primitive, but nevertheless useful hot water generator, as follows:

'I bought a 6 m long black garden hose, wound 4.5 m around a wooden frame and carried this up the ladder on to the south side of the roof of my house. The other 1.5 m I

connected to the hydrant in the yard and to the bath tap.
Through this simple arrangement we had 22 litres of very
hot water every half hour on each sunny day.'

Naturally the installations which are available commercially
today are not so simple. However, they use the same principle
and have much better efficiency.

The modern solar hot water generators consist of two main
parts: the sun collector, and the hot water store (also called the
boiler or tank). The surface collectors can heat water from 50°C
to 80°C. Vacuum collectors with selective surfaces reach an idling
temperature of 300–350°C. With parabolic radiation concentrators much higher temperatures can be produced. The various
types of sun collectors are analysed in Chapter 6.

The sun-heated water from the collectors (55–56°C) is taken
to the heat exchanger of the solar boiler (tank) which heats the
usable water content (150–500 litres). This heating is variable
according to the duration and intensity of the sunshine. The
circulation of the heated water may be on the thermo-syphon
principle (Figure 5.1) or with the aid of a pump (Figure 5.2)
which is controlled by a thermostat mounted in the uppermost
collector.

The tanks (boilers) can be made of metal or plastics and are
thermally insulated. For industrial use, when larger amounts of
hot water are required, there are also mass produced tanks of
several thousand litres capacity, e.g. for hospitals, barracks, bath
installations, camping grounds, hotels, boarding schools, etc.
The collectors can be connected in series, and the daily output
thus increased. In North Africa and the Middle East there are
installations which have a daily output of between 5000 and
10000 litres.

Larger solar hot water installations can also be found in
Europe. For example, the French firm, Sofée, has built a high
output solar installation for a hotel with thirty-five rooms and a
camping ground. In Berne, in Switzerland, an installation is in
operation which produces about 9000 litres of hot water from
40 m² of collector surface.

In some Japanese installations the sun collectors and storage
tanks are built into a single structure. In order to ensure a natural
thermo-syphon circulation, the water tanks must be at least
600 mm higher than the uppermost collectors; if this is not possible,
a circulation pump must be fitted. The connection with the house
is made by ½ in diameter (15 mm) thin walled copper pipes,
which are insulated against heat-loss. For less sunny days, an
electrical heating element of 0.5 to 2.0 kWh is provided; this
is controlled by a thermostat. The tanks and pipe system work
under a pressure of about 6 atm, and the test pressure in most
cases is 10–12 atm.

The hot water tanks are mounted either on the roof or in the
cellar. The French firm, Exenersol has developed a system in
which the storage tanks are designed as kitchen furniture and

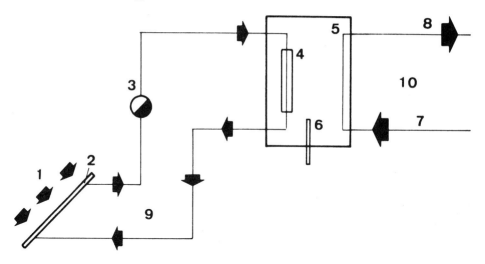

Figure 5.1
Solar heat water systems — thermo-syphon type

1. Light rays
2. Water-type sun collector
3. Thermostat
4. Heat exchanger
5. Double-skinned sun boiler

6. Electric heating element
7. Cold water inlet
8. Hot water outlet
9. Solar heat circuit
10. Usable water circuit

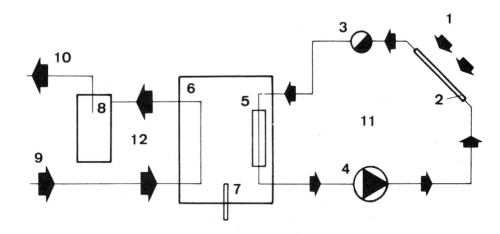

Figure 5.2
Solar hot water systems —circulation pump type

1. Light rays
2. Water-type sun collector
3. Thermostat
4. Circulation pump
5. Heat exchanger
6. Double-skinned solar tank

7. Electrical heating element
8. Auxiliary boiler for usable water
9. Cold water inlet
10. Hot water outlet
11. Solar heat circuit
12. Usable water circuit

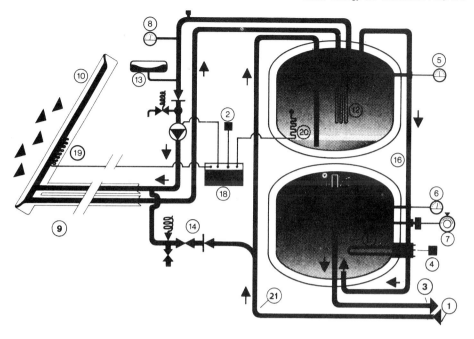

Figure 5.3
Solar hot water systems – Exenersol System

1. Cold water inlet
2,4. Electrical switches with light
     indicators
3. Hot water outlet
5,6. Thermometers
7. Controller
8. Manometer
9. Solar heat circuit
10. Water type sun collector
11. Solar hot water
12. Heat exchanger
13. Solar heat circuit expansion
    chamber
14. Safety valve
15. Usable water tank
16. Hot water section of usable
    water circuit
17. Electric heating element
18. 'Optimasol' electronic control
19. Thermostat for solar heat circuit
    pump control
20. Thermostat for double-skinned
    solar tank
21. Cold water section of usable
    water circuit

take their place in the kitchen like cookers or refrigerators
(Figure 5.3).

The French firm Sofée, already mentioned, is mass producing
dual-purpose boilers, solar-electric, solar-gas or solar-oil, which
are in use in France and Spain. For each climatic and geographical
position, there is an optimum ratio between collector surface and
solar tank volume. As a general value, Sofée estimate 35 litres/
m²/h.

By connecting the solar boiler in series with the existing boiler,
(oil, gas or electric) on the usable water side, the cold water
inlet can be pre-heated, whereby heat energy can be saved even
under less sunny conditions. When enough 'solar hot water'
is available, the oil heating is automatically switched off. Because
of the ever increasing demand for hot water, the use of solar
heated water becomes an increasingly important means of saving

fuel and money every year. In 1940 the amount of hot water used was 25–30 litres per person per day, in 1960 it was 40–60 litres and by 1980 it is estimates to be 70–90 litres. These amounts have already been exceeded in the USA. Solar energy can heat much of this water, thereby saving on other forms of energy.

It is possible for three-quarters of the year in sunny regions to produce hot water at at least 50°C by means of simple surface collectors. Even near London it was possible, during five summer months on two thirds of the days, to produce 50 litres of hot water at 55°C per square metre of collector per day.

The hot water requirement is dependent on the size of the house, the number of persons, the standard of living, occupation, age, time of year and other conditions. The required temperature varies between 30°C and 90°C, but if possible 60°C should not be exceeded, in order to avoid 'furring' and corrosion. The outlet temperature is generally between 35°C and 40°C for personal use, 55°C to 60°C for the kitchen, and 90°C to 95°C for laundry use (actual temperature, as used, about 45°C).

For a bath (full), about 150 litres of water at 40°C is required, which means 4500 kcal and requires the consumption of about 0.75 litres of oil. Today, in Switzerland, 60 litres of hot water per person per day is used on an average (3000 kcal 0.5 litres of oil). Annually, this means about 22 000 litres per person (1.1 million kcal and about 200 litres of oil).

Several Swiss-built solar hot water installations have proved that, even under average climatic conditions (e.g. Zürich, latitude 47° 30′N solar radiation 1160 kWh/m² per year, sunshine duration 1693 h/year) a large amount of hot water can be produced from solar energy.

A sun collector which converts about 70 % of the radiation energy into heat in the water can in mid-Switzerland in an average year produce more than 7000 litres of hot water at 50°C. In the Alps or in Tessin the production goes up to about 10 000 litres/m²/year.

Herr Schärer from Grenchen (Switzerland), who built a solar hot water installation with 10.5 m² collector surface, saved about 1187 litres of oil during the summer months (April to September) when the typical combined heating systems work with especially poor efficiency, 10–20 % instead of 60–80 %. On sunny days the oil heaters were switched off completely, and the average daily oil consumption through the year was reduced from 16.73 to 10.24 litres, a saving of about 6.5 litres of oil per day.

The highest hot water output in Zürich is possible in July and August, about 42 litres/m²/day, the lowest in December – about 4 litres/m²/day; By the end of February the output reaches about 20 litres/m²/day, the same as in mid October. The daily solar radiation also reaches maximum and minimum values in these months. (August, about 4.4 kWh/m²/day, December, about 0.8 kWh/m²/day).

These calculations for Zürich have assumed an average collector efficiency of about 45 %. For an incoming water temperature of 10°C this means a hot water temperature of 50°C. On the same basis, for central UK (lat. 52N), the highest hot water output is in June and July, about 45 litres/m²/day, the lowest in December, about 2 litres/m²/day. If we sum up these figures over a whole country such as Switzerland, we can see how much imported oil can be saved by the production of solar hot water.

In Switzerland, the hot water requirement of about 40 litres at 60°C per person per day can easily be provided in summer by a 1 m² collector. If each household had a 1–2 m² collector on the roof (total about 6 million m²) Switzerland could, according to the calculations of the Swiss Association for Solar Energy (SSES), save about 1 million tons of oil each year. This saving in oil represents about 10 % of the oil imports, or one third of the total electricity requirements.

According to French calculations (G. Gaillant) a normal house in France of about 100 m² area, will use in the year 2000 about 4000 kWh of energy per year (12.5 kWh/day) of this the sun could on the average provide 2000 kWh per year. The construction of only one million solar water heating installations (France has 51 million inhabitants) would save France about 2000 million kWh of energy per year.

By a similar reckoning (I. F. R. Dickinson, E.M.A. Ltd.) in the UK illustrates the case of a household of four people using a total of 150 litres of hot water at 60°C per day, which amounts to 9 kWh/day, i.e. 3300 kWh annually. In S.E. England, about 1000 kWh/m²/year of solar energy is available. Allowing for a system with 30 % average efficiency, 8 m² of collector area would provide two thirds of the household's hot water needs. This is 2000 kWh per year and thus like the French case, one million such installations would provide a similar overall saving of 2000 million kWh per year.

At the second Symposium of the 'Swiss Association for Solar Energy' at the University of Lausanne (June, 1975) some interesting figures were given for the possible saving of oil through solar water heating. Herr Madern from Perpignan gave figures which cover the average values over seven years. For an hotel in Perpignan (about 35 rooms) the following figures could be achieved per year for each square metre of collector surface:

From May to August   200 litres of oil/m²
From November to February   50 litres of oil/m²
From September to October,
    and March to April   70 litres of oil/m²

These figures signify an annual saving of oil of 320 litres/m² of collector surface. (Perpignan 2500 hours of sunshine, 1500 degree-days (see Appendix 1). It is therefore not surprising that in 1951, 50 000 solar hot water installations already existed in Florida. The saving in electric power amounted to 150 000 kWh each day.

The low oil and electricity prices of the '60's made these

installations relatively less economical, but today several million
solar heaters are installed all over the world, – 3.5 million
are installed in Japan alone. European firms are also showing
ever greater interest in this new technique, so that it is to be
hoped that the significance of these installations will be more
generally recognised.

5.2 Solar space heating systems

Almost half of all conventionally produced energy is used for
space heating (e.g. about 46 % in Switzerland). The sun shines
also in the winter, and this diffuse and direct radiation is generally
greatly underestimated.

On a December day near Zürich physicist A. Fischer was able
to generate steam; this was at the sun's lowest point and with an
ambient temperature of 3°C. One day later a solar collector of
0.7 m² surface area heated 30 litres of cold water from the
garden tap to 60°C.

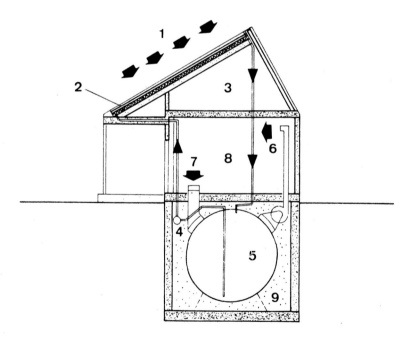

Solar space heating systems
Figure 5.4
System 'MIT 1'

1. Radiation
2. Water type solar collector
3. Thermal buffer zone
4. Circulation pump
5. Hot water storage tank
6. Warm air to living space
7. Return air duct
8. Living space
9. Insulation

43

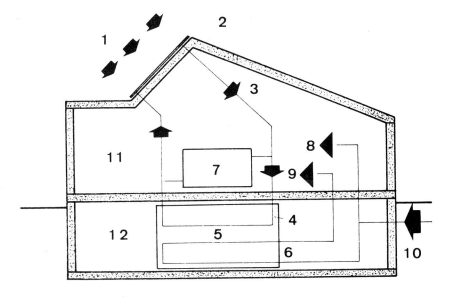

Figure 5.5
Water System (basic principle)

1. Radiation
2. Solar collector, water type
3. Hot water to storage tank
4. Solar heat circuit with heat exchanger
5. Hot water storage tank
6. Usable water circuit
7. Heating element or floor heating
8. Cold water outlet
9. Hot water outlet
10. Cold water inlet
11. Living space
12. Cellar

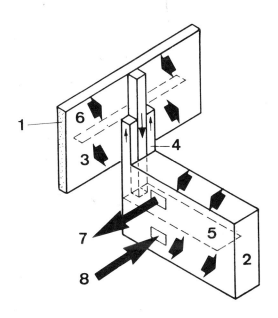

Figure 5.6
Telkes-Raymond System

1. Solar collector, air type
2. Chemical heat store
3. Direction of movement of air for taking up heat
4. Air duct
5. Separator
6. Spacer
7. Warm air to living space
8. Return air duct

Solar energy in winter can be readily applied to space heating. In mid-season periods, when there is often sunny but cold weather, solar room heating can be significant because for sudden and short temperature variations the oil heating does not have to be switched on, thus enabling the surplus energy for the running of the system to be saved.

For houses which are seldom used, and summer homes (i.e. holiday homes, bungalows, camp sites), heating by solar energy is particularly useful. In winter the rooms are warmed with free energy, and excessive cooling of the walls and damage by condensation and mildew are avoided. Very little control is needed and the natural circulation of the air keeps the building dry and immediately inhabitable. Thus the annual maintenance costs are substantially reduced. To heat a house in winter does not need much collector surface, and the same installation provides free hot water in the summer when the holiday houses and camping sites are mostly used.

Although the Greek writer Xenophon about 2400 years ago described a possible use of solar energy, the first houses in which the use of this energy was tried were not built until between 1930 and 1945. The first attempts failed because of the poor storage capability of the houses which had too many windows. Solar House MIT 1 (see Figure 5.4) built in 1939, showed interesting results (Massachusetts Institute of Technology, H. C. Hottel, B. B. Woertz). This trial building had a living space of about 46 m^2 and the 37 m^2 solar collectors were mounted on the south-facing roof, and inclined at 30° to the horizontal. The collectors worked on the water system, the absorption surfaces and the pipes were of copper, and the covering was triple glass. Heat storage was with 62 000 litres of water which by the end of the summer was heated to 75°C. The hot water warmed the air, which was circulated in the living space.

This house demonstrated the first problems of solar heating e.g. leaking water tanks, collectors broken by thermal expansion, insufficient house insulation, and costly storage units. Figures 5.5, 5.10 and 5.11 show schemes for other heating systems using water.

The main components of a solar space heating installation are:

Solar collectors (water or air-type, concentrated or not).
Heat transfer medium to the store (water, air or chemical).
Heat store material (water, stone-filling, concrete or chemicals).
Heat transfer to the rooms (water, air or chemicals).
Heat producing elements (radiators, floor heating, etc).

These units are analysed in detail in Chapter 6. The various possibilities can be combined as required.

The search for technically satisfactory and economical solutions led to hundreds of patents in all parts of the world, of which many were built and tested. These show the classical systems of solar space heating. A few of the best known are described in the following paragraphs.

5.2.1 MIT System

The very first solar house built between 1939 and 1959 at the Massachusetts Institute of Technology by H. C. Hottel, B. B. Woertz, A. G. Dietz and C. D. Engebretson, had a system operating with water, which has since become classical (Figure 5.4).

The water filled solar collectors (single, double or triple glazed) absorb the sun's heat. This warm water is pumped into stores in the cellar, and the storage water is heated by means of heat-exchangers. The hot water in the stores, heats the air, which is blown into the living spaces.

Typical example: MIT Solar House III (1949) by H. C. Hottel and C. D. Engebretson.

> Experimental building, on one level with one room. Floor area 55.7 m². Solar collectors water type 37.2 m², inclination 57° to the South, double glazing, cylindrical water storage tanks 91 cm in diameter, 9.1 m long, capacity 6750 litres. 30 % of the radiation energy was delivered to the stores. On an average 90 % of the heat requirements of the house were provided by solar energy (in the coldest month 75 % to 85 %). Autonomy of the house (independence from outside sources of energy), 2 days.

5.2.2 Telkes-Raymond system

In this system, air type solar collectors and Glauber Salts $(Na_2SO_4.10H_2O)$ stores were installed for the first time in 1948 (Figure 5.5).

The solar collectors heat air and this heat is conveyed to the chemical stores. Warm air is taken to the living spaces from the stores by means of ducts.

Typical example: Peabody House in Dover-Mass (USA) by M. Telkes and E. Raymond (1948).

> Two-storey building; upper floor, however, not heated. Air-type solar collectors, 66.9 m², mounted vertically on the South side. Heat stores of 13.3 m³ volume, filled with Glauber salts $(Na_2SO_4.10H_2O)$. Total volume of the store including air space 28.3 m³. 80 % of the heat requirements of the house provided by solar energy. Auxilary heating is electric. Autonomy of the house, 6 days.

5.2.3 Bliss-Denovan system

A house using this system with stone-filled stores was built in 1954. The heated air from the solar collectors was taken to the store, and from there was taken to the living space through a second circulation system (Figure 5.7).

Typical example: Bliss House in Amado, Arizona (USA) by R. W. Bliss and M. K. Denovan 1954.

This house was the first to be heated and cooled 100 % by solar energy.

Single storey house of 65 m^2. Air type solar collectors of 29.2 m^2, single glazing, storage by 65 tons of pebbles filling (volume 36 m^3) in the basement, electrical auxiliary heating was provided for but not needed. In summer, the house was cooled by the same system. Aesthetic and architectural problems were not solved, but the correctness of the system was proved. This system has also become classical, and has since been often built with variations and sometimes improved.

5.2.4   Löf system

The first system with air-collectors and gravel stores was used in the Boulder-house built in 1945. Heating was by hot air distribution. The heat store can be placed either horizontally or vertically. (Figure 5.8).

Typical example: Löf House in Denver Colorado (USA) 1959.

The house has a living area of about 186 m^2. The air type collectors are mounted on the roof at 45° to the South, 55.7 m^2. The air, warmed in the collectors, is taken by a 1 h.p. motor to the store, which consists of two vertical cylinders (91 cm diameter, 5.5 m high) filled with 6 tons of

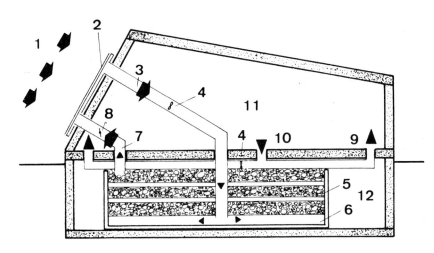

Solar space heating systems
Figure 5.7
Air System (basic principle)

1. Radiation	7. Cold air return
2. Air type solar collector	8. Regulating valve
3. Warm air to the store	9. Warm air to living room
4. Fan	10. Cold air return
5. Stone filling (bed)	11. Living room
6. Air space	12. Cellar

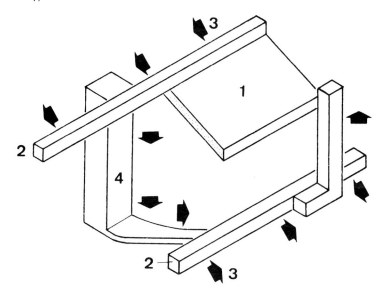

Figure 5.8
Löf System

1. Air type solar collector
2. Warm air transport (ducts)
3. Movement of air for taking up heat
4. Heat store with stone filling

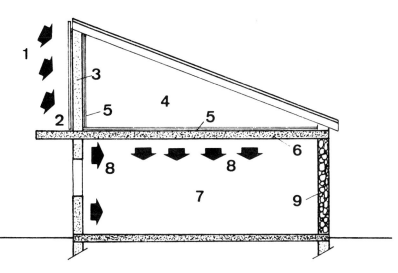

Figure 5.9
Lefever System

1. Radiation
2. Glass
3. Storage wall, outer surface black
4. Thermal buffer zone
5. Insulation
6. Heat storage ceiling(s)
7. Living room
8. Heat output
9. Insulating wall to the North

granite. Air is blown through this hot granite filling and taken into the living space. In winter about 25–30 % of the necessary heating energy and a part of the hot water requirements are supplied by solar energy. During the summer special single-glazed collectors provide energy for cooling purposes, and double-glazed collectors produce hot water.

5.2.5 Lefever system

This very interesting and simple system was used for the first time in 1954. The walls of the building are heated by vertically-mounted solar collectors, and serve as heat stores (Figure 5.9). By this means the usually very expensive heat stores are eliminated and the solar heating system thereby made cheaper.

Typical example: Lefever House in Stowerstone, Pennsylvania (USA) by H. R. Lefever (1954).

Two storey house, of which only the ground floor was heated (area 116 m²). Air type solar collectors (area 41.8 m²) are mounted vertically on the upper storey, facing South, and are double-glazed. No special heat stores. Storage is in the walls. The living rooms are heated by warm air circulation. About 40 %–50 % of the total heat requirements of the house are provided by solar energy. Auxiliary heating by gas.

5.2.6 Morgan system

This first European system was built in 1961 near Liverpool in England. The building is heated only by solar radiation and some auxiliary sources (human heat, lamps). There are no solar collectors in the usual sense, and no stores, as the heat is stored in the walls and celings of the building (see Figure 9.1).

Typical example: St. George's School in Wallasey (Liverpool, England) by A. E. Morgan (1961).

The School building for 320 pupils is 67 m long and has two storeys. The south side is 90 % glass and behind the glass panes is a black-painted concrete wall. The concrete ceilings and various brick walls are of such a size that they can absorb much heat, store it, and radiate it again later. There is no auxiliary heating, and the additional heating required is produced by human heat and electric light. The autonomy of the building is 7 days. Measurements made by the University of Liverpool (M. G. Davies) show the heating system to be very satisfactory (see also Chapter 9, section 9.2).

5.2.7 Trombe-Michel system

This French solar house system (Patent CRNS Trombe 1956) stores the solar energy only in the mass of the building (Figure 9.3), similar to the Lefever System. The solar radiation is absorbed by vertical, south-facing triple glass surfaces, which are mounted on a black concrete wall (30—40 cm) (Glass surface is 10 % of the volume of the building). The heated air passes through small openings into the living space and distributes the heat by natural convection. The first experimental house using this method was built in the Pyrenees in 1962.

Typical example: 'Solar Chalet' in Odeillo by F. Trombe and J. Michel (1968).

This 'solar chalet' has a living area of 80 m² (on one level). The whole south face (except for a double door) is covered with solar collectors. As the climatic conditions in Odeillo are very good (2750 hours of sunshine), 3600 degree-days). 0.5 m² of collector surface is sufficient for each 10 m³ of building (Paris 1 m² per 10 m³, Chauvency le Chateau 1.3 m² per 10 m³). The heat requirements of the house amount to 32 000 kWh/year, 65 % of which is produced by solar energy. The auxiliary heating is electric. Energy autonomy of the house, 2 days.

5.2.8 Sky-therm system (Hay-Jellott)

In this system, built for the first time in 1967, there are no solar collectors or heat stores in the usual sense. The collection and storage of the solar energy is done by a water trough 21 cm deep, mounted on the flat roof. The trough is made of black polythene units, which can be covered by hard polyurethane sheets 4.5 cm thick. At night in the winter the water trough is covered, and the house is heated through the ceiling. In summer the trough is left open at night, is covered during the day and

Figure 5.10
Solar house in Odeillo
with vertical collectors

cools the rooms (Figure 5.15). This effect is brought about by radiation and evaporation.

Typical example: Sky Therm House in Phoenix (USA) 1967.

Experimental building on one level with one room. House area about 11 m². Area of water trough collector 15.8 m². The building was tested for two years, and the results were very satisfactory. A bigger house is being built in Atascadero in California (USA).

5.2.9 Baer system

The main point to note in this system is that ninety containers each of 200 litres capacity are integrated into the South wall of the house. (Total 18 000 litres of water). When the sun is shining, the black painted outer surfaces are uncovered, and the solar radiation falling on them through a glass screen heats the water (Figure 6.5). At night and in bad weather the surfaces

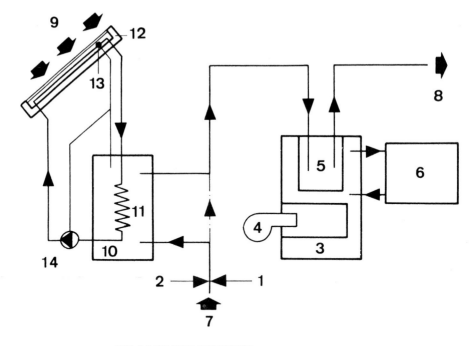

SOLAR HEATING SYSTEMS
Figure 5.11
Solar heating installation as auxiliary to oil heating (H. Rüesch)

1. Existing oil heating
2. Auxiliary installation
3. Duel purpose boiler
4. Oil burner
5. Hot water boiler
6. Radiator or floor heating
7. Cold water inlet
8. Hot water outlet
9. Radiation
10. Double-skinned solar boiler
11. Heat exchanger
12. Water type solar collector
13. Thermostat for pump control
14. Circulation pump

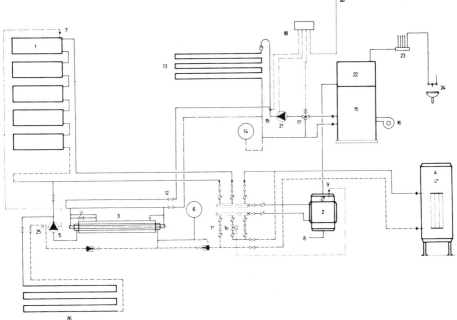

Figure 5.12
Solar heating system (R. Schärer)

1. Solar collector
2. Double-skinned solar boiler
3. Heat exchanger for room heating
4. Store for surplus heat
5. Circulation pump for charging current circuit
6. Expansion for charging current circuit
7. Thermostat for pump control
8. Cold water inlet, usable water
9. Thermostat
10. Magnetic valve overflow control
11. Discharge valve, overflow store
12. Cut off valve
13. Floor heating
14. Expansion chamber
15. Alternative combustion dual purpose boiler
16. Oil burner
17. Mixing valve
18. External temperature control
19. Output sensor
20. External sensor
21. Circulation pump, room heating
22. Double-skinned dual purpose boiler
23. Hot water distributor
24. Hot water outlet
25. Interconnecting switch
26. Installation for melting snow

are covered from outside by movable units (sheets of hard insulation) and give up to the living room the heat taken in during the day.

Typical example: Baer House in New Mexico (USA) 1972.

The house has a living area of 185 m² (one level) and a net collector area of 24.1 m². The house is heated 90 % by solar energy, the remaining 10 % being provided by two wood burning fires. In summer the 'water walls' are cooled by the night air, and during the day are used for air conditioning the house. The movable outer walls are 35 cm thick, weigh only 6.75 kg/m² and have a high insulation value. The auxiliary heating (two fireplaces) is only needed about ten times per year.

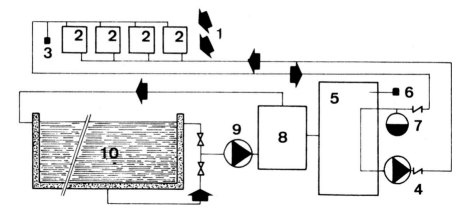

Figure 5.13
Schematic diagram of a solar swimming pool heating system

1. Radiation
2. Water type solar collector
3. Thermostat for charging pump control
4. Circulation pump
5. Solar double-skinned boiler
6. Thermostat for heat exchanger
7. Expansion
8. Filter
9. Filter pump
10. Swimming pool

5.2.10 Bridgers-Paxton system

This system was developed in 1956 and was one of the first in which heat distribution by floor heating was achieved. The heat intake is with water collectors. The storage and heat distribution medium is water. This system is used almost exclusively today by European manufacturers.

Typical example: Bridgers-Paxton Office building in Alburquerque, New Mexico, USA.

The building is heated and cooled with solar energy. It has a useful area of about 410 m². The solar collectors, using water, are of aluminium and have an absorption area of 71 m². The heat store consists of 23 000 litres of water. The heat output is achieved by water filled pipes which are integrated into the floors and ceilings. The installation is also provided with heat pumps. The solar system has been functioning satisfactorily since 1956.

Figure 5.14
Passive solar heating system (Wagner)

1. Radiation
2. Space, heated by greenhouse effect
3. House wall

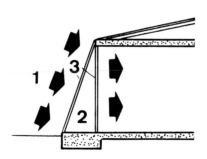

5.2.11 Wagner system or passive use of solar energy

In this type of building the solar radiation is converted directly into space heating. There are no solar collectors, but the house is partly or completely contained in a cover of transparent glass. The space between the house wall and the outer glass is heated by the 'greenhouse' effect. The structure of the house is usually used as part of the heat storage arrangements.

Typical example: 'The Growing House' by M. Wagner.

This building designed in 1931 has a living space of about 94 m^2. The living room is the centre of the building and the other rooms are arranged around it. The house is surrounded by a glass skin which gives an intermediate space about 1.5 m wide, where the 'greenhouse' effect occurs. This idea also applies to the Autonomous Solar House being studied in Cambridge, already mentioned.

5.2.12 Other systems

Naturally there are a very large number of other systems which sometimes allow for substantial improvement in detail. The many patent offices all over the world could name thousands. Modern solar heating systems are often fitted with heat pumps and sometimes with solar cells, which still further increases the number of possible combinations. In most cases the principles and main elements remain the same as those installations described above.

The possibility of using solar energy for space heating relatively soon is very optimistically estimated in several countries. According to G. Gaillant, Engineer of Electricité de France, France could save about 5000 kWh of electricity per house in the year 2000 by building a million solar houses. This would mean an annual saving of about 5 billion kWh. If water and space heating are considered together, a 7 billion (10^9) kWh (7000 kWh per house) could be saved annually, which could mean 0.7 % of the total electric power requirements for France in the year 2000. The actual possibilities are still much greater.

In America in the 'Solar Energy Panel' by R. Cherry and M. Morse already mentioned, 35 % of the heating and air conditioning of buildings by solar energy is anticipated for the year 2035. By 1985 two million barrels of oil could be saved daily by solar heating.

Experiments in Turkmenia (in the Soviet Union) have shown that the additional costs for building fitted with a 'solar system' (heating, 300 litres of hot water per family per day, and cooling in summer) amount to about 4–6 %. This can be amortised in a relatively short time through savings in electric power and oil.

Unfortunately, the all important ratio between building costs and solar energy has not been investigated in detail. The main problem is that for every climatic condition and for each building, different optimum figures apply. Scientists and engineers are still not agreed on the optimum solar engineering methods.

For the Swiss Lake of Geneva region the Battelle Institute in Geneva (J. C. Courvoisier and J. Fournier) have made interesting calculations concerning the use of solar energy for room heating. For Geneva, Lausanne and Neuchâtel, the annual oil requirement for room heating amounts to about 3043 litres (Leysin 5650 litres).

The calculations have shown that also with average radiation conditions (hours of sunchine annually: Geneva 1979, Lausanne 1971, Neuchâtel 1699, Leysin 1808) fairly large savings of oil are possible.

For a house with 120 m² living area and 50 m² collector area (efficiency 70 %) 48 % of the annual oil requirements can be saved in Geneva (1463 litres), 52 % in Lausanne (1583 litres), 41 % in Neuchâtel (1245 litres) and 47 % in Leysin (2650). Reckoned over the whole country, this saves enormous quantities of oil which are not burnt, thus saving money and preserving the environment.

5.3 Cooling by solar energy

At first sight it seems a paradox to provide a cooling medium from the sun's heat. But by the use of solar energy there is a whole range of possibilities, from room cooling to the production of ice.

A building which must be air conditioned in summer, under normal European weather conditions, often results from a method of construction which has not been rationally thought out.

In warmer countries, i.e. North Africa or the Middle East, houses can be built so that the rooms remain cool naturally. There are innumerable examples of this in traditional architecture. However, if air conditioning is required, the possibility exists of using solar energy quite readily because on hot days, when the energy for cooling is needed, the maximum radiation power is available, and thus the problem of energy storage does not exist. Rooms can be cooled naturally by solar energy, i.e. simple natural processes can be used, such as the evaporation of liquids, or energy can be produced for conventional cooling processes.

5.3.1 Natural space cooling (cooling effect by the evaporation of water)

It is a known physical phenomenon, that by the evaporation of a liquid, heat (the latent heat of vaporisation) is taken out of the surroundings and thus a cooling effect produced. Hay and Jellott have used this effect for the air conditioning of buildings in their 'Sky Therm' system already mentioned.

On the flat roof is a layer of water 21 cm deep, which is left open at night in the summer and produces cooling by radiation and evaporation (Figure 5.15). By day the water layer is covered with a hard polyurethane sheet 4.5 cm thick, to cut off direct solar radiation. The cold water on the roof cools the living space through the ceiling. (Examples are the Sky Therm House in Phoenix, USA, by Hay and Jellott 1967, Solar House in Atascedro, California, USA, by Hay 1975). The house in Phoenix was tested and evaluated as very good.

The problem with the above system is that in many hot countries, where air conditioning is really necessary, water is rare and expensive. This makes the running costs for the use of water fairly high.

5.3.2 Space cooling by inverted 'greenhouse' effect

With solar collectors working on the 'greenhouse' principle, everything has been done to increase absorption, and to reduce heat losses, reflection and re-radiation. To be able to cool, i.e. to reduce the intake of heat, we can take the opposite measures. These are:

Reduce direct irradiation by suitable orientation of the building.
Assist natural re-radiation.
Use surfaces which are transparent to thermal radiation (e.g. layers of Polyethylene).
Selective reflecting surfaces on the roof and walls (aluminium, glass, water, plastics layers, white finish).
Thermal insulation.

These measures can be combined; for example, painting the outside of a wall white, and having the inner surface of aluminium. Experiments have shown that by similar methods internal temperatures can be attained which are 10° to 20°C lower than the outside temperature.

5.3.3 Solar energy for conventional cooling processes

Conventional processes make cooling possible by the evaporation of a liquid, which is put under pressure. Ammonia (solution) which has a very low boiling point, is often used as a fluid. This process requires energy, which under certain conditions can be obtained from solar energy (Figures 5.15 and 5.16).

The French research institute (CNRS) built an experimental installation in the Pyrenees, which, using a focussed collector, produced 25–50 kg of ice per day. There is also the possibility of converting solar energy directly or indirectly into electric power, and using this to operate conventional cooling equipment.

In the Soviet Union Orif Chodiev built a solar refrigerator, in which the fluid was replaced by a solid substance. This substance evaporated under solar radiation without becoming fluid, and took a crystalline form, whereby a cooling effect was obtained. This solar refrigerator works without a compressor. With an increase in ambient temperature more ice is automatically produced.

According to experts, the wider use of solar cooling installations could come more quickly than that of heating, as the maximum radiation is there when it is really needed, and thus

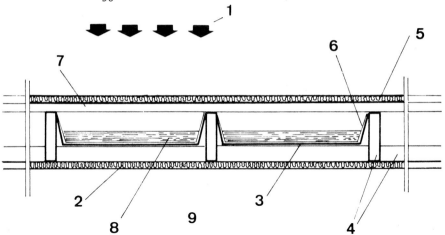

SOLAR SPACE COOLING SYSTEMS
Figure 5.15
Natural solar space cooling system (Hay-Jellott)

1. Radiation
2. Roof insulation
3. Plastics elements
4. Roof structure
5. Movable plastics elements

6. Black plastics container
7. Metal rails
8. Cold water
9. Living space

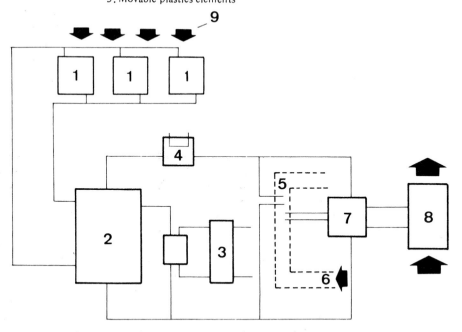

Figure 5.16
Solar energy for conventional air conditioning installation (L. W. Butz)

1. Solar collectors
2. Main storage
3. Usable water boiler
4. Auxiliary heating
5. Air ducts

6. Air inlet
7. Absorption conditioning
   installation
8. Cooling tower
9. Radiation

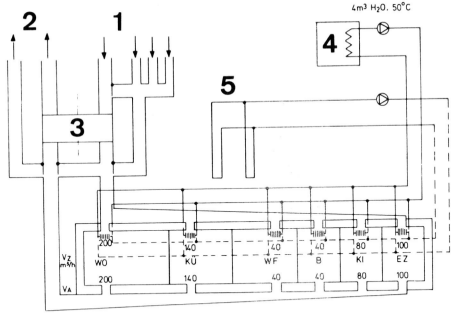

Figure 5.17
Solar space cooling principle (Philips)

1. Fresh air porous wall
2. Air outlet
3. Econovent. This is a two-way air vent with simple heat exchanger between ways so that warm outgoing air passes heat to otherwise cold incoming air
4. Hot water and usable water store
5. Underground heat exchanger

the expensive storage problem is eliminated. In Virginia USA, NASA as part of their research programme are constructing a building of $18\,000$ m^2 which will have a collector area of 5000 m^2. All the energy necessary for the air conditioning of this building will be obtained from solar energy.

5.4 Swimming pool heating with solar energy

An ideal possibility is offered to owners of swimming pools to use solar energy, as these installations are used mostly in fine weather. In the USA where relatively many people own their own homes, a private swimming pool is no longer unusual. The use of solar energy in this field is also no longer a novelty. Today, there are already over a million solar swimming pool installations in use.

E. A. Farber, Director of the Energy Conversion Laboratories at the University of Florida, has made comparative experiments with traditional and solar heated swimming pools. The experiments have shown that the solar heating works effectively, mainly if the system is connected to the general solar heating system of the house. With this arrangement the water temperature can be maintained at $22°$C above the ambient air temperature.

There are many systems on the market; one of the best known in the USA is that of the Burke Rubber Co (San Hosé, California). The solar collectors consist of flat-shaped black plastics containers (Du Pont-Hypalon) which are usually mounted on the roof. A pump raises the water from the pool to the collectors, and after heating it returns to the pool by natural thermo-syphon circulation. The collector elements are of standard size (2.4 m X 2.4 m and 2.4 m X 3.6 m) and cost approx. 130 dollars and 162 dollars respectively. The installation is guaranteed for ten years.

One American firm offers a 'Do-it-yourself' swimming pool installation for 19 dollars which under normal conditions can heat 45 000 litres of water.

The greatest problem with solar swimming pool heating is the large heat loss at the water surface. Since 1955 Brooks, Löf, Root, Czarnecki and others have tried to find methods of reducing this heat loss. Today many of these pools, when not in use, are covered with a large plastics sheet which is treated with thin layers of p.v.c. (Czarnecki). This allows the solar radiation to pass through and acts as an insulator against loss of heat to the outside (solar collector operation). If only a medium water temperature is required, this method helps to prolong the swimming season, without additional solar collectors, and at the same time helps to keep the water clean.

The first European solar installation for swimming pool heating was produced by Brown Boveri (Mannheim, Germany) and (see Figure 4.6). Previously the open air bath in Wiehl was heated in Germany. Previously the open air bath in Wiehl was heated by an electric filter heater, and needed about 700 000 kWh of energy for the season (May to September). This installation was replaced by a new form of solar heating which warmed the water to 24°C. The electrical power required (for operating water pumps and heat pumps) was at the most, about 70 000 kWh for the season (10 % of the previous requirement). A space of about 1500 m² was required for the installation of the solar collectors. To make space available for additional use, the collectors were installed in the form of a hall. The auxiliary heating needed for periods of inclement weather, serves as a cooling system for an ice rink, which is built in the hall.

The method of operation is as follows. From October to May the ice rink is in use; in the cold months of November/December to February/March the energy taken from the ice rink heat-pumps is used to heat the hall. In the transition time April/May and September/October the heat not needed in the hall is taken to the open air bath, which makes possible a swimming season from about April to October. The annual power requirements for the ice rink and swimming bath together are no more than that previously required for the swimming bath heating alone. The project cost 12 million DM (£2.7 million) and was financed 80 % by the Government.

6 The Basic Elements of Solar Engineering

The main functions of a solar heating system are the absorption, transport, storage and giving back of heat. These functions are performed by many different elements (conduits, boilers, controls, etc) as in a conventional heating system, but the main elements, which are specifically for a solar system, are the collector and the heat store. These two elements comprise the main problem of a solar heating system, and it can be said that a solar installation is only as good as its collectors and stores. These latter are joined by a heat transport system.

A possible auxiliary element in solar heating is the heat pump.

6.1 Solar collectors

The purpose of the solar collectors is to capture the sun's radiation with as high an efficiency as possible. There are different types of collector according to shape of the outer surface, formation of absorption surface and the 'collecting' medium.

Solar collectors for space heating in the winter, under unfavourable irradiation conditions, must also be able to convert a substantial amount of the incoming solar radiation into useful heat. They should heat up to a working temperature of between 60-90°C with an ambient temperature around freezing point. At this temperature the collectors give up about 70 % of the incoming solar radiation as heat to a liquid (or a gas) which acts as a heat transport medium. Collectors are chosen according to the purpose for which they are required; they can be either flat collectors which absorb unconcentrated, i.e. direct or diffuse sunlight, on the the one hand, or tubular, strip, sheet or hollow collectors, which convert into heat direct solar radiation concentrated by optical means, on the other.

When exposed to the sun, the flat collectors, which are specially important for the European climate, represent a heat source of

Figure 6.1
Integral solar roof
(Zinco)

large area and low energy density. The collector must be carefully insulated on both sides if it is to function correctly.

Two firms, Brown Boveri and Co. (Mannheim) and Philips A.G. (Aachen) have completed one year's experiment and have published the results. In several places, including Bregenz (Vorarlberg) and Heidelberg, Brown Boveri determined the amount of energy it was possible to obtain. The experimental installations were fitted with 1.5 m² surface collectors. According to the average values obtained, it can be calculated that in Germany the amount of energy available will provide about 80 % of the hot water requirements in summer, about 20 % in winter, and 65 % between seasons.

The above figures are naturally dependent on the climatic and technical conditions (total collector surface, storage volume, insulation, efficiency of the system etc.).

The Brown Boveri surface collectors were installed for the first time for heating the open air swimming bath in Wiehl — 3000 m²

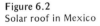

Figure 6.2
Solar roof in Mexico

collectors heat the water to 24°C. This project, carried out under commission from the German State Ministry for Research and Technology, was the first large installation for the use of solar energy in Western Europe. The experience gained from this can also be evaluated for the provision of private swimming pools (see Chapter 5).

Philips Research Laboratory GmbH have developed high efficiency focussed collectors, which were installed for the first time over a larger area in the Experimental Energy House in Aachen.

Other systems such as Stellar, Alcan, etc are also already on the market. In the UK, USA, France and Germany many more varieties of solar collector are available.

6.1.1 Focussed collectors (radiation concentrators)

These collectors have a concave surface. A typical example is shown in Figure 6.3. They concentrate the sun's rays by mirror or lens effect. 200°C to 500°C can be obtained by weak concentration (1:10). With higher concentration temperatures up to 4000°C can be obtained.

For heavy industrial or research purposes, the solar concentrators form part of solar furnaces or solar power stations. The solar furnace in Odeillo-Font-Romeu (French Pyrenees) has a parabolic mirror system 40 m high and 54 m wide (focal length 18.4 m). A temperature of 4000°C is attained (maximum thermal power of the installation is 1000 kW), and is used for melting experiments.

Large radiation concentrators have also been built in the USA, Japan, Australia, Algeria, Greece, Soviet Union, and other countries. The concentrating collectors, also called mirror collectors, must generally be controlled in direction, and are very susceptible to soiling by dirt or dust which could spoil the optical quality. It

Figure 6.3
Solar heating installation with focusing and flat surface solar panels

is possible to protect the mirror against the effect of the weather by a glass cover, but the glass, unlike surface collectors, must be cleaned very frequently, in order not to reduce the direct radiation by further scattering.

Radiation concentrators can normally only use direct radiation. But the latest research has shown that, in spite of this disadvantage such collectors can be installed for mid-European climatic conditions and for domestic purposes.

The solar collector built by the Philips Research Laboratory GmbH is fitted with a heat reflection filter of Indium oxide (In_2O_3), which has a transmission for sunlight T = 85 %, and a reflection for heat radiation R = 90 %. The collector has an absorption factor for sunlight of 95 %.

A few values of actual efficiencies for the Philip's collector with additional cover are given below. The values were obtained experimentally in a water heating application in the summer. (Water temperature 50°C above ambient).

Weather conditions	Total radiation W/m²	Efficiency %
Cloudless sky, clear	800	61
Thin cloud, hazy	600	58
Thin cloud cover	300	45
Cloudy	150	20

Liebi, Neuenschwander and Co. (Berne, Switzerland) also produce focussed solar collectors, which consist of numerous cylindrical parabolic mirrors. The direct radiation normal to the mirror, is concentrated on a tube fixed in the focal line, and through which flows the liquid to be heated. To avoid heat transmission losses, the concentrated energy is transferred directly to the inside of the tube which, for this purpose, is transparent. There is an internal black absorber which transfers the received energy to the heat-carrying medium by convection.

In the UK, Natural Power Systems Ltd. is developing parabolic focussed solar collectors, in which a cylindrical parabolic reflector rotates about a tube at the focus line, following the sun. The tube, carrying the circulating liquid, is blackened for absorption of radiation and shrouded by a concentric glass tube to reduce heat losses.

The next few years will show which types of collector are the most economical.

6.1.2 Surface collectors

Surface collectors have a flat absorption surface and their operation is based on the 'greenhouse effect'. These consist of a frame
(plastics, metal or wood), transparent sheets (single, double or
triple, glass or plastics), absorbing surfaces (selective or non-
selective), insulation and a heat transporting medium (air, water,
oil, glycol etc).

The characteristic selective outer surfaces for modern solar
collectors were first produced experimentally by Prof. H. Tabor
who achieved with a suitable combination of two thin layers,
solar radiation absorption values of 94 % combined with a relative
emission of 6 %. All these elements together form a solar radiation
absorbing device which is cooled by the heat transfer medium.
The incoming solar energy can be only partly used, part is lost
through reflection, absorption or leakage of the constructional
elements.

A good surface collector for a temperature range of up to
100°C should have the following properties:

Can be mounted firmly in a structure.

So long as only medium operating temperatures are required
it should have an efficiency of not less than 50–60 %.

For lower temperatures an efficiency of 70–80 % should be
obtainable (for higher temperatures, 20–30 %).

The materials used for insulation and/or the casing of the
collector itself, should have as low a heat conductivity as
possible. This is so that after the beginning of what is
perhaps a short period of solar radiation, the collector
operating temperature can be reached as quickly as possible.

The outer surface of the heat insulation must be stable under
all atmospheric conditions.

The main heat losses of the collectors are caused by:
- dirt;
- shadows from holders and parts of the frame;
- reflection losses from glass covers;
- transmission losses in the glass;
- radiation losses transmitted out through the glass covers
  resulting from heat losses through conduits of the
  absorption surfaces. (They are proportional to the
  difference between outside and absorption layer temperatures, and can therefore be represented by a K-value for
  the collector);
- heat conversion losses from the absorber to the cooling
  water;
- convection in the layer of air between the collector surface
  and the glass cover;
- heat conducted through the cover glass supports or sealing,
  and in the air between the collector and the glass cover.

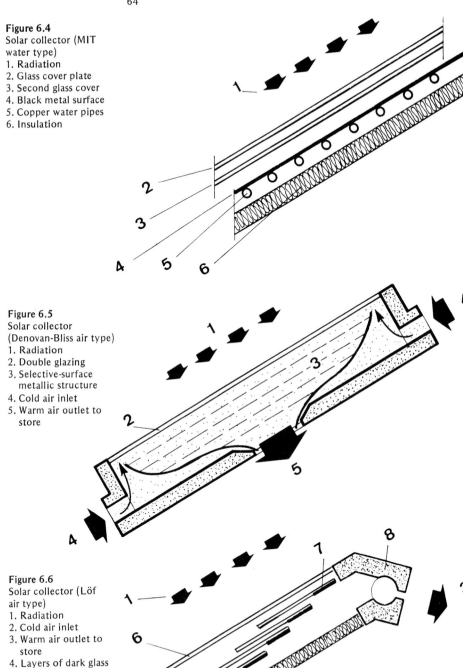

Figure 6.4
Solar collector (MIT
water type)
1. Radiation
2. Glass cover plate
3. Second glass cover
4. Black metal surface
5. Copper water pipes
6. Insulation

Figure 6.5
Solar collector
(Denovan-Bliss air type)
1. Radiation
2. Double glazing
3. Selective-surface
   metallic structure
4. Cold air inlet
5. Warm air outlet to
   store

Figure 6.6
Solar collector (Löf
air type)
1. Radiation
2. Cold air inlet
3. Warm air outlet to
   store
4. Layers of dark glass
5. Insulation
6. Cover
7. Black surface layers
8. Frame structure

The ratio between incoming radiation energy and useful heat energy output gives the efficiency of a collector. The highest temperature which can be obtained with a collector, is reached when no further usable heat is taken out of it through the heat transfer medium. That is, when input radiation energy is equal to collector losses plus usable heat extracted. This is called the 'idling' or equilibrium temperature.

Different idling temperatures are obtained according to the design and quality of the collector, the radiation intensity and the ambient conditions. In mid-Europe 800 kcal/h in sunshine can be considered a normal value. With this radiation a single-glazed collector can produce a temperature of about 100°C, while with triple-glazing about 190°C can be obtained, but typical flat plate collector working temperatures are 70–80°C.

The efficiency of a collector can be increased by special treatment of the glass covers, panes, sheets and of the absorption surfaces. A collector with an efficiency of 70 % can be regarded as normal in a typical low grade heat case.

The size of the absorption surfaces is dependent on how much heat is required, how the collectors and the house are designed, and the geographical and climatic situation of the installation. For an 80–100 % supply of hot water in mid-Europe 7–10 m² of collector per house would be sufficient if adequate energy storage was possible. For room heating a surface of between 30 and 150 m² is required according to insulation and climatic situation and the capacity of heat recovery available from the storage. The inclination of the collectors is calculated generally

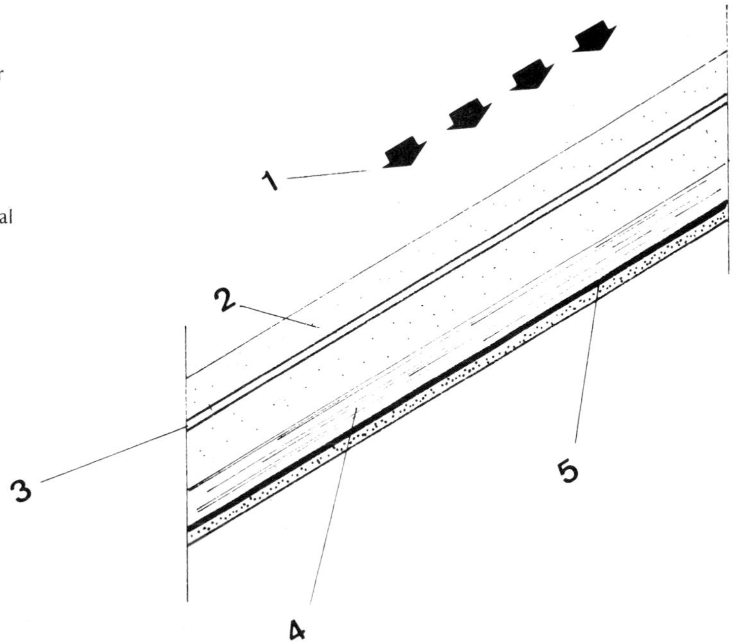

Figure 6.7
Oil type solar collector
(Alexandroff)
1. Radiation
2. Roof frame
3. Transparent cover
4. Oil
5. Black, selective metal
   surface

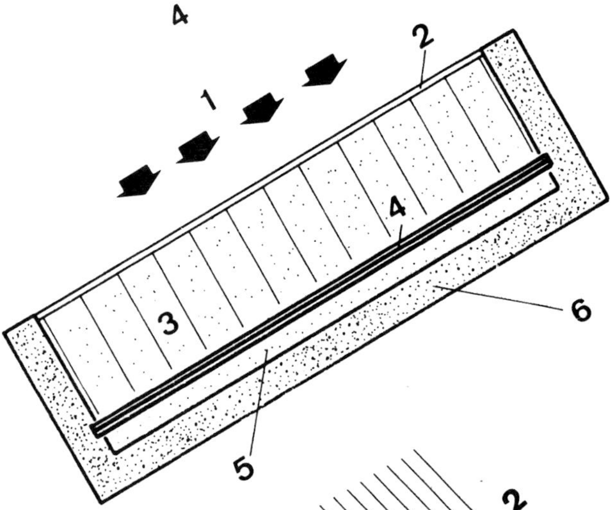

Figure 6.8
Air type solar collector
(Francia)
1. Radiation
2. Transparent cover
3. Hexagonal prisms of
   thin plastics material
4. Selective surface
5. Insulation layer
6. Frame structure

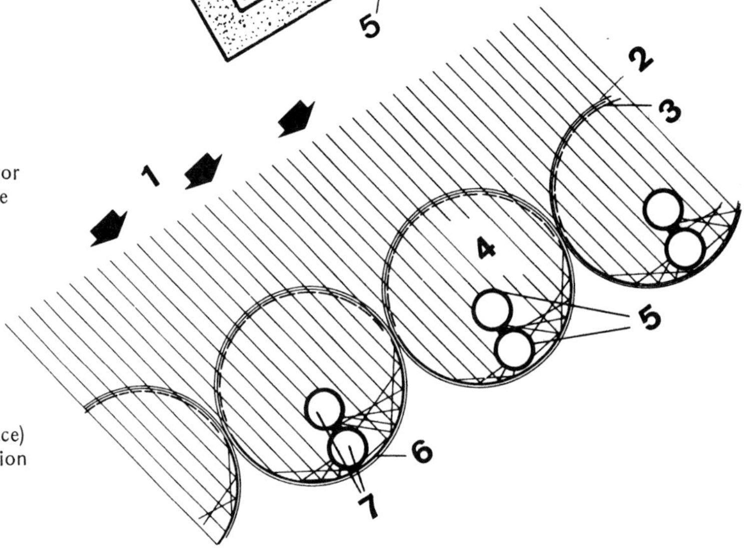

Figure 6.9
Radiation concentrator
(focusing), water type
(Philips)
1. Radiation
2. Glass cover tubes
3. Heat reflection
   filter
4. Vacuum
5. Absorption tubes,
   black vitreous
   enamelled
6. Silver mirror (surface)
7. Hot water circulation

for winter conditions (see Figures 6.10 and 6.11). Values obtained from experience are:

Inclination = Latitude + 10° to 15° (referred to the horizontal)

If the collectors are required only in the summer then

Inclination = Latitude − 15°

The best known 'classical' collectors are:

Water type — MIT (Figure 6.4).
Air type — Denovan-Bliss (Figure 6.5).
Air type — Löf (Figure 6.6).
Oil type — Alexandroff (Figure 6.7).
Air type — Francia (Figure 6.8).

Apart from these now classical collectors, other models, which often provide interesting improvements (e.g. Figure 6.9), are being introduced. Solar collectors which work in summer and winter

under the most severe climatic and thermal conditions are subjected to many hazards, which must be considered in the design.
The most important problems which can be met by a solar collector are:

Overheating;
Danger from frost;
Corrosion;
Dirt;
Breakage;
Thermal movements of expansion/contraction;
Leakages.

These hazards can vary in degree according to the climatic
conditions and the remedies vary from one model to another. The
collectors should carry a guarantee of quality and the manufacturer
should have the technical performance such as efficiency, heat
values, etc approved by an official organisation.

6.2 Heat storage systems

The main problem in the use of solar energy for central heating
purposes is that, in general, most solar heat is available in the
season when least heating is required. Conversely heating is
required when there are few hours of daily sunshine. So to be
able to use the solar energy when really needed, it must not only
be collected but also stored so as to be capable of recovery when
required. With an ideal storage system the energy of the sun
would be available day and night, summer and winter.

Heat from the sun can also be used without storage, if the
amount received is sufficient. If the requirement is for more heat
than the sun can provide, the solar heat can be used to supple-
ment the energy from other sources, e.g. oil. A 'short-term'
store can hold energy for from a few hours to several days, but
in this case considerable auxiliary heating is still required.

Using a solar heating system with short term storage means
that about 50—70 % of the energy can be saved, according to
climatic situation and engineering construction. With 'long-term'
storage the surplus heat from the summer can be stored for the
winter. A heat store can hold energy by an increase of its 'sensible'
heat; that is by raising its temperature. The sensible heat being
the product of the specific heat, the mass and the temperature
change.

Utilising the sensible heat of liquids or solids results in the
internal energy of the system being altered by increasing the
kinetic and potential energy of the molecules of the storage
substance. Greater internal energy changes can result from
changes of state of the substance, e.g. transition from the solid
phase to the liquid phase. In this case, the internal energy of the
storage system is altered by the equivalent of the 'latent' heat
which corresponds to the change of state e.g. the latent heat

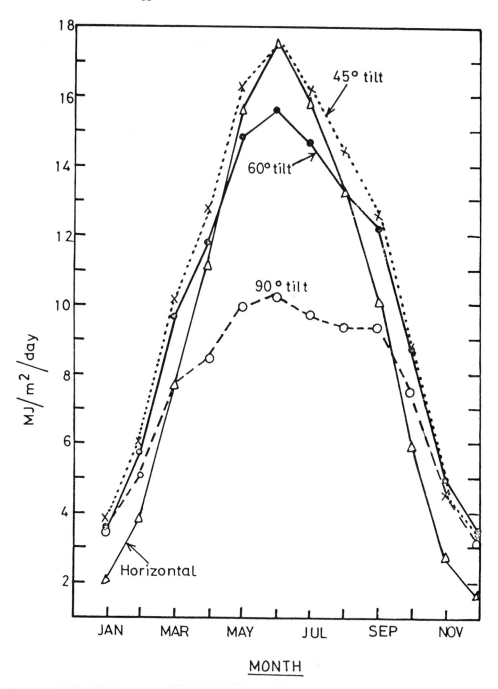

Figure 6.10
Mean monthly values of total irradiation on slopes of 45°, 60° and 90° at Kew compared with horizontal surface. Estimated from horizontal surface data 1957–1971. (Reproduced by permission of UK-ISES)

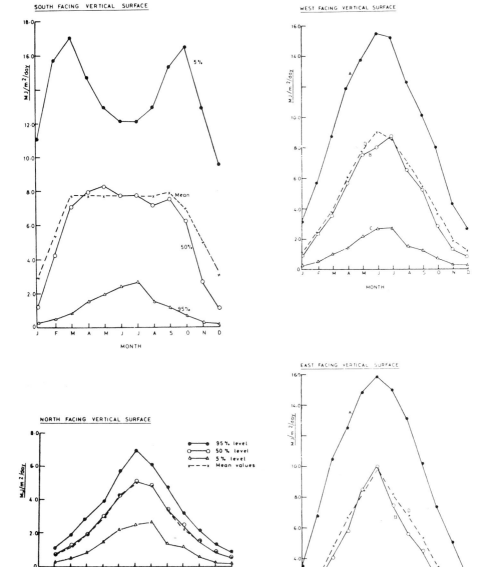

Figure 6.11
Mean monthly values of daily vertical surface irradiation at Bracknell,
exceeded on 5% of days — lowest full curve, on 5% of days — highest
full curve on 50% of days — full curve in middle, and also overall monthly
mean shown by dotted line. Ground reflected radiation is excluded by using
appropriate shading devices. (Reproduced by permission of UK-ISES)

of melting or of evaporation. Heat stores may therefore be sub-divided into sensible heat types and latent heat types.

In most countries the cheapest heat storage medium is water and this has the highest specific heat. The following are a few heat storage values for materials expressed as specific heat measured in $kcal/m^3/°C$.

	$kcal/m^3/°C$
Brickwork	320 – 360
Concrete	450 – 600
Sand	308
Stone(s)	475 – 588
Water	1000

The most important criteria of quality in the choice of suitable types of storage are:

How much heat, when and at what temperature must the store deliver?
What heat losses occur during the storage time?
How much space does the store need?
How must the store be constructed so that it costs as little as possible for a given power?
What is the ratio between storage and external energy input?

In order to be able to solve this problem of storage economically, which is simple in principle but still very expensive, various possibilities are being examined world wide. For example, a well-insulated house in Switzerland (400 m above seal level) requires about 15 to 22 Gcal of energy per year.

Part of this energy can be provided by winter sun and through heat pumps, so that according to P. Kesselring's calculations only about 6 Gcal of the solar energy in the summer need be stored for the winter. However, specialists are still not at all in agreement over the necessary storage volume. The performance of a system giving independence in periods of bad weather is related to the climatic conditions prevailing and varies from 6 hours to 10 days. It is naturally more difficult and expensive to achieve two days self sufficiency in Denmark than ten days in the Canary Islands. Depending on the heating system employed there are several possibilities for heat storage. Water or pebble (stone) filling can be used. Also the surrounding soil is sometimes used as a storage medium.

Heat storage is always a relatively expensive problem. To keep the price down, systems have been devised in which no separate storage volume is necessary. In the Lefever, Morgan and Trombe-Michel systems, the building structure stores the heat, whereby the cost of the whole solar installation is substantially reduced. In Japan solar hot water installations are in operation in which the collectors and stores are combined.

6.2.1 Hot water stores

Hot water stores are the most common forms of storage. Many experts consider hot water to be the best form of storage, although the problem of corrosion can present a few difficulties. To avoid heat losses, the water tanks must be well insulated. Water and pebble (stone) stores are sometimes used in combination. 1 m³ of pure water stores 1000 kcal/°C.

The temperature range over which the water can be used begins at 70–80°C and finishes with use of heat pumps at about 4°C. According to A. Fischer, a well-insulated single-family house with about 200 m³ of hot water can store enough energy from the summer into the winter, bearing in mind the continuing input in autumn, winter and spring. The usable heat content of a store is less than its capacity, because in the time between storage and use, heat is lost to the surroundings. The time constant of the loss is dependent on the controlling geometrical and material parameters, such as:

Storage volume and surface area.
Thickness of insulation.
Specific heat of the storage fluid.
Heat conductivity of the insulation material.

If a certain amount of heat is to be available over a given length of time, there are various storage methods which are possible. One can use a small, very well insulated store, or a large store with a shorter time-constant, i.e. higher losses. The question is: What is the optimum? The optimisation problem is defined by the cost parameters, and also by the charging conditions at the beginning and end of the storage period. The most important factors are:

Cost per cubic metre of the storage structure.
Cost per cubic metre of the insulation.
Minimum usable storage temperature.
Temperature difference between the store and ambient.
Duration of storage period.
Amount of heat which must still be available after a certain
    length of time.

By careful design for a given application, the storage parameters can be so optimised that the costs of installation are minimal. If possible the heat given up to the surroundings (storage losses) should be to the advantage of the house i.e. retained within the house. It is also an advantage to stratify the heat store into say three different temperature levels, which together are available for three different purposes. For example, domestic water at 50–80°C, water for floor heating 30–50°C and water below 30°C as the input to the solar collectors.

At the end of the autumn charge all three compartments are, of course, heated together to about 80°C, and hold the full storage capacity for use at the beginning of the winter season.

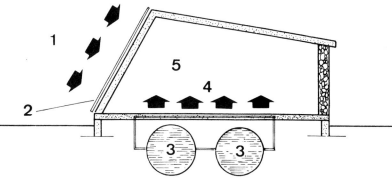

HEAT STORAGE SYSTEMS (WATER STORAGE)
Figure 6.12
1. Radiation
2. Water type solar collector
3. Underground, insulated water tank
4. Heat output through floor heating
   or radiators
5. Living space

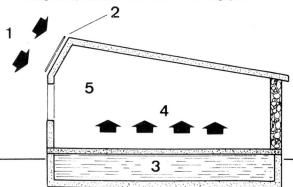

Figure 6.13
Hot water store under floor
1. Radiation
2. Water type solar collector
3. Water in insulated concrete tank
4. Heat output
5. Living space

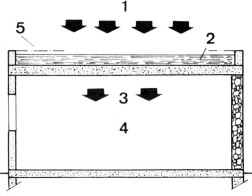

Figure 6.14
Storage with layer of water on the roof surface (Hay-Jellott System)
1. Radiation
2. Layer of water in black plastic
   channels
3. Heat output
4. Living space
5. Movable cover(s)

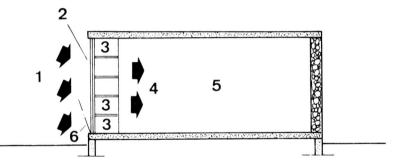

Figure 6.15
'Water-Wall' as a heat store, by S. Baer
1. Radiation   4. Heat output
2. Glass pane(s)   5. Living space
3. Twenty containers each with   6. Movable cover(s)
   200 litres water (outside black)

The first solar house, MIT 1, built in Cambridge, USA in 1939, stored the summer solar energy for the winter. The house had a living area of 46.5 m^2 and a water store of 62 m^3 (See Chapter 5, Figure 5.4). Figures 6.12 to 6.15 show various possibilities for storing heat by water.

6.2.2 Stone-filled stores

At a small material cost, stone, coarse gravel or rubble (such as concrete or brick) provide relatively good heat capacity. However, these materials need more storage volume on account of the small temperature range which is available with normal flat solar collectors, or which is desirable for good efficiency.

Although the material cost can almost be neglected, the cost of the container and the required storage space, and also of the charging and discharging arrangements must be considered. The transfer of heat is here generally very simple; with 'solid-material' stores, air flows directly through the layers of stone, or through ducts in concrete stores, and is heated or cooled. (See Chapter 5, Figure 5.9). The charging and discharging of these stores, with continually varying temperatures, requires an automatic control which suits the strongly fluctuating system. These stores are already being investigated theoretically and experimentally all over the world (Figures 6.16 to 6.19).

With a 30 % air space (porosity) and with three times the weight, stone has only a third of the volumetric storage capacity compared with water. Often stone stores end up requiring four times the volume of a water store of the same capacity. The stones usually have a diameter of about 5 cm and less for high temperatures. 1 m^3 of stone can store about 400 kcal/$^\circ$C.

In 1945, George G. Löf built the first solar house (Boulder House in Colorado) in which the heat storage was with 8 tonnes of gravel about 5 m^3.

6.2.3 Chemical heat storage

In 1944, Professor Maria Telkes of the Delaware University produced a storage system with Glauber Salts ($Na_2 SO_4 . 10H_2 O$). By increasing the temperature from 27°C to 38°C this salt is able to store at least eight times as much heat as the same volume of water over the same temperature range.

Glauber salt melts at 38°C and the heat absorbed is given up again upon solidification. The cost of providing such a store is higher than that for water, but there is a saving in volume and insulation material. The Glauber salt is unchanged and does not need renewing. For the Peabody House in Dover (USA) built between 1944 and 1948, Glauber Salt to the value of 3000 dollars was needed, and the house could be heated for from six to ten days with stored solar energy.

In 1961 Maria Telkes carried out a cost comparison for an average house with 75 6000 kcal of heat to be stored. The figures are given in Table 6.1.

Table 6.1 Cost comparison of latent heat stores with water and stone storage (Heat to be stored 75 600 kcal)

	Water	Stone	Latent Storage
Necessary volume m³	4.53	7.93	0.71
Weight kg.	4536	22 680	998
Container cost @ 28.25/m³ dollars	128	0	20
Construction space @ 42.38/m³ dollars	192	336	30
Material cost (dollars)	0	25	20
Total cost (dollars)	320	361	70

These results are, however, certainly too optimistic, as, for example, the price per unit volume of the container for the latent heat store and for the latent heat store chemical, are taken to be the same. There are still some difficulties to be overcome in this type of system and many other chemicals are being investigated. For example, Philips at Aachen have selected potassium fluoride tetrahydrate for study. Important criteria of quality in the choice of a suitable chemical are:

High value of heat storage per unit volume.
Good heat transfer ability in the charged and discharged states.
Small change of volume.
Chemically stable.
Low corrosion effects.
Low cost.

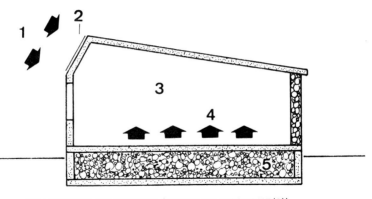

HEAT STORAGE SYSTEMS (STORAGE BY STONE(S))
Figure 6.16
Stone filling under the floor
1. Radiation
2. Solar collector
3. Living space
4. Heat output
5. Stone filling in insulated storage space

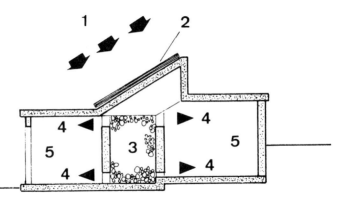

Figure 6.17
Heat storage with a stone-filled store as a 'Central Stove' (Sun Mountain System)
1. Radiation
2. Solar collector
3. Stone filled store with insulation
4. Heat output
5. Living space

Figure 6.18
Heat storage with concrete storage walls
(Trombe-Michel System)
1. Radiation
2. Glass pane
3. Thick concrete wall as a store (black outside)
4. Warm air to living room
5. Cold air to the collector
6. Living space
7. Air outlet
8. Layer of air

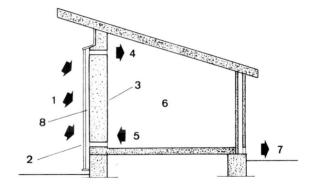

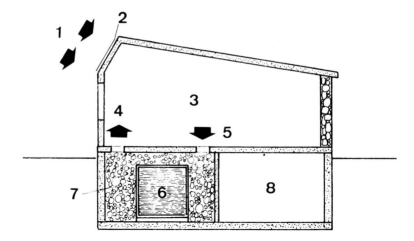

Figure 6.19
Mixed storage with stone filling and water (Thomason System)
1. Radiation   5. Cold air return
2. Solar collector   6. Hot water tank
3. Living space   7. Stone filling
4. Warm air to living space   8. Cellar

For stores which use latent heat there are hydrated salts which melt in their water of crystallisation and can thereby take up much heat of melting and hydration. There are many of them at low cost, available in part as 'additives' (see Appendix 1). Many other substances can, of course, be used as latent heat store materials, including organic compounds, especially paraffin wax.

Latent heat stores can absorb considerably more energy per unit volume in the lower temperature range than can pure 'capacity' stores. Chemical stores have more than five times the storage capacity than hot water stores of the same volume. In comparison with a stone store the latent store is superior in this respect by a factor of nine.

According to J. I. Jellott, the cost of these storage materials, including 'additives', is about £25 per tonne. However the not inconsiderable cost of containers for these sometimes reactive materials, and also of 'surfaces' through which the heat is conducted, must be added to this.

Many specialists are inclined to think that the future lies in latent heat stores, but which storage system is the best is still an open question. In a few years a large number of installations will provide figures which will simplify the decision.

6.3 The heat transfer system

The heat absorbed by the solar collectors must be taken to the stores and from here to the living space. Water and air are the main forms of transfer media.

6.3.1 Water

As water flows through pipes, the heat output is through floor heating or special radiators. The main problem of the water system is corrosion; however, it is used more often than air because it is thermally more effective.

About 10 to 40 litres of water per hour per square metre of collector surface circulate between the collector and the store.

6.3.2 Air

With the air system the chief advantage is that there is no corrosion problem, but the collector temperatures and storage volumes must be greater, and the cost of the system is thereby increased. A volume (of air) of about 0.3 $m^3/min/m^2$ collector surface between collector and store is reckoned.

In special cases, where no separate store is necessary (i.e. the Lefever, Morgan and Trombe-Michel systems) the air system can be financially advantageous.

6.4 Heat pumps

In many solar houses an important auxiliary element — the heat pump — is added to the solar heating system.

The heat pump is a heating system which enables available unused and free sources of heat to be used for heating purposes, and thereby reduces the load on the solar heating system. The principle of the heat pump was described by the English physicist Lord Kelvin in 1852.

Heat pump installations take heat from surrounding water at low temperatures. The source may be 'ground-water', rivers, streams, lakes, the soil, air and drainage water. This free heat is transformed to a higher temperature and thus made usable for heating and the production of hot water. On days without sunshine this system gives worthwhile assistance to the solar installation. Heat pumps make the solar house much more independent of periods of bad weather, but it must be remembered that they require an external energy supply.

The first solar house fitted with heat pumps was built in New Haven (USA) in 1950. The solar office block, by Bridgers and Paxton (Albuquerque USA 1956) also operated with heat pumps. Today many modern solar houses such as Solar-One House (Delaware, USA) are fitted with this system.

Some experts debate whether heat pumps are really necessary for solar heating installations.

7 Design and Basic Calculation of the Solar House

Although solar energy is available in very large quantities, its use is made difficult by its diffuse distribution (only 60 W/m² in winter) and by the irregularity of the radiation (day/night, summer/winter). The harnessing of the energy and its storage demand relatively large capital investment, thus solar energy, in the same way as gas or electricity, must be regarded as 'quality' energy.

7.1 Design rules for the solar house

By careful building design (orientation, insulation, etc) the energy requirements must be kept as small as possible. A solar house should be designed basically as such, and this concept carried through to the smallest detail.

The following are the most important rules, which should always be kept in mind:

To build with understanding of the climate and to recognise the dependence on natural conditioning.

An installation wasteful of energy is only trying to improve a bad building design, mostly without success and always uneconomically.

By good insulation of all parts of the building, to reduce the energy requirements of the house.

To choose a K-value for walls and roof not greater than 0.5.

To reduce window area to a minimum, and to choose at least double, and if possible triple glazing.

To position openings and solar collectors on the south side, and to orient the building correctly.

Avoid shading the south facing side(s).

To integrate the solar collectors and heat stores into the architecture aesthetically and in a satisfactory manner technically.

POSSIBILITIES FOR INTEGRATING THE SOLAR COLLECTORS INTO
THE BUILDING STRUCTURE

Figure 7.1
Solar collector integrated into the
roof structure

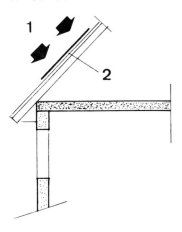

Figure 7.2
Solar collector as terrace (balcony)
space

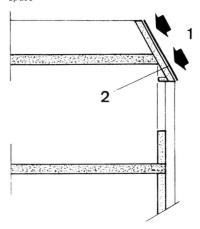

Figure 7.3
Solar collector as window breast

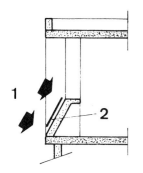

Figure 7.4
Solar collector as 'shed element'

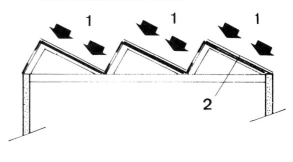

Figure 7.6
Solar collector as part of the structure
1. Radiation
2. Solar collectors (facing south)

Figure 7.5
Solar collector as wall element (unit)

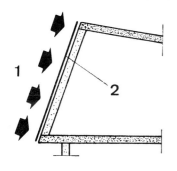

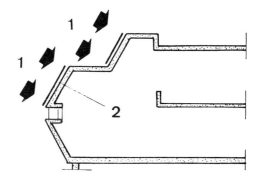

Figures 7.7 to 7.12
1. Radiation
2. Solar collectors (facing south)
3. Solar boiler (double-skinned)

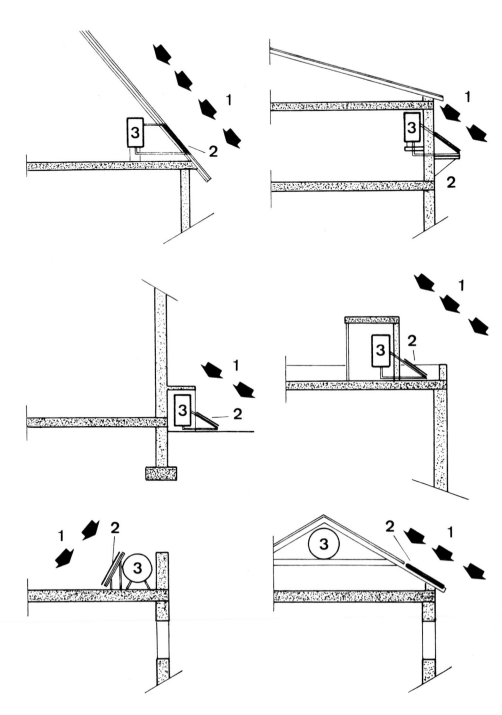

By technical and constructional means to re-use energy already used in the house (waste-water, lighting, etc).

Protect the house from cold winds (by trees, slopes, thermal buffer zones, etc).

In windy regions to provide power generation by windmills.

To optimise the ratio between building volume and outer surface (maximum possible volume for the least surface).

To design thermal buffer zones (i.e. double doors, sheltered terraces, etc).

To utilise the physical phenomenon of 'rising heat'.

To utilise the thermal storage properties of the building with a view to optimising the storage and recovery of heat to suit the day/night and seasonal cycle of heat energy demands.

To optimise the ratio between comfort, autonomous energy and external energy.

To reduce the window losses by increasing the K-value. (A window provides us with fewer calories by day than it loses by night. If the windows are insulated by night, a positive heat balance can be achieved for a south facing window.)

To include in the energy balance, available energy such as radiation through the windows, lighting, human and animal warmth.

To utilise heat generated in the kitchen by means of special stove with large storage capability, and by constructional measures.

To avoid shading by other structures.

To provide the bathroom and kitchen on the north side, and regard them as buffer zones.

By partly underground rooms to use the heat storage capability of the soil.

If these rules are followed as far as possible, the intake in the energy balance will be relatively large, and the losses small. By these and similar measures the energy requirements of a given living space can be reduced to 50 % of present typical levels.

7.2 Calculating the requirements for the solar house

The principal sequence of operations for the calculation of requirements for a solar house is as follows:

1. Design the layout and volume of building so that the largest space content is obtained for the minimum area of outer walls. Provide maximum openings to the south, determine the advantageous positioning of solar collectors, and define good insulation values for walls, roofs and windows. Meteorological tables and local insolation intensities are already available for most areas.

2. Calculate the heat losses for the space heating requirements.

The most important heat losses are:
Loss through outer surfaces.
Loss through ventilation.
Storage losses.

3. With the help of the 'Degree-Day' concept (see Appendix 1) determine the monthly heat requirements dependent on outside temperatures, i.e.

'Degree-Day' × outer surface × K-value = heat requirement

4. Calculate the amount of energy necessary monthly for the production of hot water (To heat 200 litres/day from 10°C to 60°C requires 280–310 Mcal/month).

5. Make a list of energy intakes concerned, and determine the monthly availability of the energy sources such as:

Total radiation on the collectors.
Radiation through the south windows.
Human heat output (about 130 Mcal/month).
Cooker heat output (about 120 Mcal/month).
Heat output from lighting (about 80 Mcal/month).
Auxiliary heat from heat pump(s), wood, fires, electrical appliances, etc.

6. Define the necessary comfort, storage and external energy strategy, and determine the most economical ratio between these factors in order to be able to fix the dimensions of the collectors and stores.

7. Determine the definitive figures for the amount of energy which is available monthly from solar radiation and other sources.

8. Establish the monthly energy balance for the energy requirements, determine the values of external energy for December/January, and try to use the surplus of summer solar energy. This can be done by swimming pool heating, production of hot water, or economical storage for use in the winter.

The main problem is the dimensioning of the collector surfaces and storage volumes, as these two elements determine the independence of the house from external energy sources. This independence, calculated for the worst winter month can have any value from a few hours to several weeks. At this point the debate over the economics of the use of solar energy begins as the stores and collectors are capital investment and cost money. At present there is no agreement on costs by the solar energy experts; 'Scientifically' calculated figures can vary by a ratio of 1 to 5 according to what one would like to prove!

It is not practical to discuss here the economics of solar heating as the facts and figures which apply today, will no longer be valid in the near future (due to possible oil price increases, cheaper solar construction elements through mass-production, etc) and will no longer be important. To reduce the problem of solar energy to a simple question of capital investment, illustrates a way of thinking which cannot or does not wish to understand the true meaning of this gift. The investment comparisons can only concern relatively unimportant problems such as money, while the most important arguments for solar energy, such as health, independence and availability of the energy, or quite simply Life on our Earth, are not to be expressed in mere figures. Sooner or later these facts will have to be generally recognised.

8 Solar Town Planning and Legal Requirements

'The main element of city planning is the human need for sun, living space and green parts, its main problem is to make these sources of human happiness available to everyone.' So wrote Le Corbusier about the CIAM Congress of 1933, at which these elements were expounded as the Doctrine of Modern Architecture (Charter of Athens).

Unfortunately, these ideas, which had arisen as a reaction to the unhealthy living conditions of the industrial cities, have been largely ignored over the last 30 years. The results of the new architecture were, in the main, the direct opposite to those which the pioneers had imagined. Instead of logical and air conditioned buildings with natural and pleasant sunshine, concrete and glass boxes with a large and uncontrollable energy demand were built.

It would be simple, of course, to make the architects and engineers responsible for this situation, but, they can only build what is demanded of them. Architecture was and is always the mirror of an Age, and our buildings are just like us. Here lies the problem: if we would like to have better architecture, we must first change our own way of thinking. Architecture, which is dependent on it, will certainly follow this change. After many decades the building industry has, today, for the first time the possibility of offering something new. Through solar architecture we can return to a healthier, pollution-free and more economical method of building, which could offer immeasurable benefits for the whole of humanity.

Urban planning is an expression of existing laws. Solar city planning needs new laws, which are related to the new technical hypotheses.

The building regulations concerning the use of space, building styles, size of windows, safety, etc must be modified in order to establish a basis for 'Solar Law'. Such legal basis already exists in England, and in Florida the law says that all new hot water installations should also operate from solar energy.

8.1 Aesthetic considerations

The discussion over the aesthetics of solar houses would fill many pages, but it is possible to produce pleasing buildings even with black solar collectors. Millions of buildings have been erected in concrete, glass and metal which have no beauty at all. The worst solar architecture is at least technically satisfying, and that is an advantage which only a few buildings of the last decades can show. It is possible to integrate solar collectors and heat stores aesthetically into their surroundings but this should not be left to the contractors. There are plenty of examples of bad, improvised solutions. This integration must be achieved for new buildings and for reconstruction, because the buildings which are standing today will form about 80 % of those still standing in the year 2000.

The public is always very conservative, compared to pioneers who would like to do something new. To win over the distrust, attempts should be made to offer the new elements first in conventional form. The first motor car builders worked on this principle with great success!

8.2 Design of solar collectors

Solar collectors can very often be designed to be invisible or built into the roof, and are thus much less 'aggressive' roof structures than some television aerials, chimneys or ventilators. We can hope, therefore, that the public and the law-makers will not oppose these new building elements. Figures 7.1 to 7.12 show examples of how solar components can be integrated into the structure of the building. Governments should encourage better building insulation and the use of solar energy by tax advantages and laws as is already done in the USA, Germany and France. The energy saved is to the advantage of the whole nation, not only in the form of saved expenditure, but also as a cleaner environment. By the use of solar energy the 'thermal ceiling' (i.e. the overheating of our atmosphere which can be caused by other forms of energy) can be avoided.

If the temperature over the whole world is raised only a few degrees Centigrade, our whole natural climate can be destroyed. Incalculable catastrophes can follow, such as reduction of air movements (without wind large cities would be immediately stifled!). Withdrawal of the glaciers, raising of sea-level, movement of the continents and other effects can be produced. Law-making must always consider the use of publicity, it must not lose time over aesthetic or other less important problems, when it should be aimed at avoiding such real and great dangers.

8.3 Solar Cities

At present there are relatively few Solar City projects. The two best known are those of Professor Giovanni Francia (Genoa) and Professor Guy Rottier (Nice). In the project, Sun City, by Professor Francia for 100 000 inhabitants, put forward by the team Amirifez, Bertalotti, Maresco, Pagano, all energy-consuming functions, such as production of hot water, room heating and air conditioning should be carried out by solar energy. The rays of the sun are reflected by mirror systems into the interior spaces which are thus illuminated. The size of the proposed storage systems provides a considerable independence from every form of external energy, even on sunless days.

The Ecopolis project by Guy Rottier was conceived with the help of Professor Maurice Tonchais and Henri Bouttier, solar engineer, and was introduced for the first time at the 1971 COMPLES-Congress (Coopération Méditerranéenne Pour L'energie Solaire). The project was in the form of hillside terraces, in which the interior spaces were illuminated through 'light corridors' (Lumiduc). The focussing solar collectors are mounted at the outer ends of the corridors and project the sun's rays into the interior of the building(s) where they are used for lighting and heating purposes.

Ecopolis is a city whose internal spaces are lit by projected solar rays. The dwellings which form about a third of the volume are built on the outer surface of the 'hill'. Inside the buildings are gardens, communal rooms, work places, businesses, shops, service installations and traffic ways.

These two projects, which contain some phantasy, but are worthy of debate architecturally, show the possibilities and problems which exist for solar city building.

To prepare productive urban building plans for the next century needs the cooperation of scientists, engineers, architects, politicians, law makers, contractors and the general public. The exercise is difficult, but the solution, must and will be found.

9 International Solar Projects

9.1 Bridgers-Paxton office buildings in Albuquerque (New Mexico, USA)

Project: Miller, Stanley, Wright.
Calculations: F. H. Bridgers, D. D. Paxton and R. W. Haines.
Built: 1956.

This installation was claimed to be the first in the world to heat and air condition office buildings (Figure 9.1). The installation which is fitted with heat pumps, is still in operation today and delivers practically 100 % of the energy required for heating and air conditioning.

The building has a useful area of 410 m², and the solar collector area amounts to 71 m². The collectors are of aluminium ('Roll-Bond') and the pipes are integrated into the absorption surfaces. Glazing is with single window glass, and the absorption surfaces are not selective. The collector surface is made of fifty-five sections fitted together, and is inclined at 60° to the South.

INTERNATIONAL SOLAR PROJECTS
Figure 9.1
Bridgers-Paxton office building, Albuquerque (USA 35° .05 ′N.)
Useful area: 410 m²
Solar collector surface: 71 m²
Hot water storage: 23 m³

The heat-transfer medium is water and heat output is by floor and ceiling heating. Heat is stored in an underground water tank (1.5 m diameter) of 23 000 litres. The autonomy of the store is three days. The installation is fitted with four heat pumps, which also effect the cooling of the building in summer (amount of cooling water 7.5 tonnes).

The cost of the approximately 4.2 m high building (volume about 1678 m^3) amounted to about 58 500 dollars in 1956, of which the installation costs for water, heating and air conditioning were about 17 400 dollars. These costs were at that time as high as the production cost of a conventionally air conditioned building. The system is still operating satisfactorily, nineteen years after installation. The technical performance was measured by Pennsylvania State University.

9.2 St. George's School, Wallasey (England)

Project: A. E. Morgan.
Built: 1961.

This school building, previously mentioned in Chapter 5, is one of the oldest, largest and best solar buildings in Europe (Figure 9.2). This solar house, which absorbs and stores the solar energy in its well-designed structure, has been in operation for fourteen

Figure 9.2
St. George's School, Wallasey (England 53° 26'N.)
1. Radiation
2. Concrete storage wall (outside black)
3. Glass panes (500 m²)
4. Heat from lighting system
5. Heat stores (concrete floor)
6. Human heat output
7. Laboratory
8. Classrooms, total 1367 m²

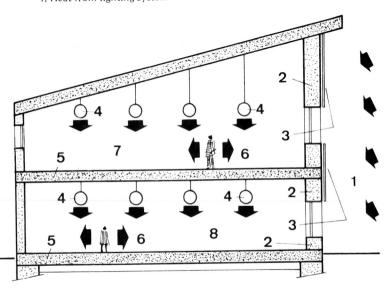

years and in spite of the less favourable climatic conditions, requires practically no external energy for its heating.

The amount of solar energy in summer is 120 W/m²/day. Human heat output is 21.5 W/m²/day and the lighting provides 38 W/m²/day.

Paradoxically, the main difficulty is that there is often too much solar energy available, which cannot be used. An auxiliary heating system was originally installed, but this was not needed, and was subsequently removed. This relatively simply built school (without separate collectors or storage system) shows that the use of solar energy is possible also for larger buildings and under relatively indifferent climatic conditions.

9.3 Solar House in Chauvency-le-Château (France)

Project: J. Michel, F. Trombe.
Built: 1972.

This solar house was built in Lothringen, where there can be 1700 hours of sunshine per year. It has a living area of 106 m² and a volume of 275 m³ (Figures 9.3 and 9.4).

The solar collectors from the Trombe-Michel (Anwar) System are arranged vertically and have a total area of 45 m². The house, which is not totally insulated, has an average K-value of 0.9. In addition to the solar heating an electrical auxiliary heating system is installed.

The rooms are heated to 18° to 20°C, which takes about 18 000 kWh of solar energy per year, of this about 10 000 is effectively used. The electric auxiliary heating requires about 7000 kWh annually.

Figure 9.3
Solar house in Chauvency-le-Château (France 49° 10′N.)
1. Radiation
2. Glass ('Triver') 45 m²
3. Layer of air
4. Concrete storage wall (outside black)
5. Warm air to living space
6. Cold air inlet
7. Warm air circulation in room
8. Air outlet
9. Steel tube roof structure
10. Living space (106 m², 275 m³)

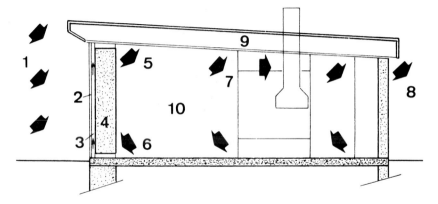

The house was produced to French dwelling construction standards. The method of construction is a steel tube frame with standard sections 3.6 m X 3.6 m. The black heat storage wall fitted with vertical collectors forms the south face. The glass surfaces are of 'Triver'. Calculations have shown that the sun delivers heat energy two to three times more cheaply than conventional heating. Heat transfer is by natural heat circulation.

The largest side of the house with the solar collectors faces south. On the north side is the water service zone which acts as an insulating heat buffer. The heat storage units are integrated into the load-bearing structure. The 'storage wall', about 35 cm thick, can store about half the incoming solar radiation, and produces a warm air circulation in the living space which lasts until the next morning. This 'solar wall' is economical, in so far as its cost of construction hardly exceeds that of a normal wall.

Michel and Trombe are of the opinion that a 'heat autonomy' of more than one day is no longer economical. The ratio between collector surface and building volume should be about 0.16 for a normally insulated house (K = 0.9 to 1.0). If the house is well insulated (e.g. K = 0.5) the ratio can be reduced to 0.1, i.e. with a 1 m^2 Trombe-Michel vertical collector 10 m^3 of building volume can be heated. For the house in Chauvency-le-Château the ratio is 45:275 = 0.163. This ratio is, of course, also dependent on the climatic conditions.

Experiments show that it is not economical to attempt to heat a Trombe-Michel house exclusively with solar energy. The optimum is between two-thirds to three-quarters of the total energy requirement. The storage walls cost about 300 francs/m^3 and deliver heat at 6 centimes per kWh, which is three times cheaper than from the French electricity supply.

Figure 9.4
Solar house in
Chauvency-le-Château
with vertical solar panels
and semi-direct solar
heating system
(G. Michel and
F. Trombe)

9.4 Solar House 'Foire de Paris 1975' (France)

Project: J. Michel.
Built: 1975.

Since 1973 various prototypes of solar heated houses have been exhibited at the Paris Fair. The 'Sun House 1975' produced by Jacques Michel, is something new in this field which is so important for our future energy economy (Figure 9.5). This privately built house is the first in Europe in which the energy requirements are provided mainly by solar and wind energy.

The house has a living area of 160 m² and a volume of 485 m³. The structure is of wood, and the walls of light building sheets with a good insulation value (K = 0.35 kcal/m²/h/°C). The solar radiation is absorbed in collectors of 45 m². The collectors, which are already produced in quantity in France, are mounted on the south side and are filled with water. The sun-heated water from the collectors is pumped to a heat store (volume 3000 litres) which, with the help of a heat-exchanger heats a solar boiler filled with domestic water. The hot water in this second circuit circulates through the radiators. In case of insufficient sunshine an electric storage heating system comes into action automatically. Light and power are delivered by fourteen solar cells and a wind-generator (Eolien). According to the builders,

Figure 9.5
Solar House 'Foire de Paris 1975' (France 48° 52'M.)
1. Solar cells
2. Solar collectors, water type (45 m²)

the solar cells deliver 14 kWh, and the Eolien 11 kWh of stored energy.

The heating system costs 36 000 (Swiss) Francs, i.e. about 21000 sF. more than normal oil heating. But for this additional expenditure it is possible to save 50–70 % of the cost of energy, according to insulation quality and climatic conditions. The solar cells are fairly expensive—sF 900 each (£215) size about 25 × 35 cm.

9.5 Philips Solar House, Aachen (Germany)

Project: Philips Research Laboratory GmbH.
Built: 1975.

On the 5th June 1975 at the Philips Research Laboratory GmbH in Aachen, the first German Solar House was introduced to the public (Figures 9.6 and 9.7). This was built by cooperation between state and private research establishments.

Figure 9.6
Philips solar house in Aachen (Germany 50° 30′N.)

1. Radiation
2. Solar collectors, Philips type (20 m²)
3. Long term heat store (42 m³ 95°C
4. Drainage water tank (1 m³)
5. Domestic hot water tank 4 m³ 45°C to 55°C
6. Heat pump (Input 1.2 kWh, output/input/ratio 3.5/1)
7. Hot water outlet
8. Living space 116 m² 290 m³

9. Lobby
10. Process controller
11. Air inlet (300–600 m³/h)
12. Air outlet (300–600 m³/h)
13. Town water
14. Waste water
15. Electric supply
16. Soil heat pump (Input 1.2 kWh, input/output/ratio 3.5/1)
17. Radiator

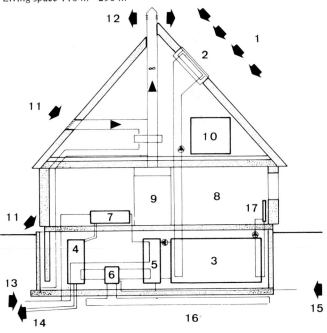

The house has a living area of 116 m² (volume of living space 290 m³) and is four to five times better insulated than a conventional house. (K (outer wall) 0.17 kcal/m²/°C, K (windows) 1.9 W/m²/°C). Through these good insulation values, a very small heat requirement was achieved i.e.

Heat conduction losses about 6300 kWh/year
Ventilation losses about 2000 kWh/year (about one-third to one-sixth less than in normal houses)

The Philips focussed solar collectors have an area of 20 m² and are built up of 324 elements. They produce low temperature heat up to 95°C. This energy is taken to a 42 m³ water tank, which can store about 10 000 to 12 000 kWh long term, to provide the total heat requirements of the house. The heat store is insulated with 25 cm of rock wool, and its temperature range is from 5°C to 95°C. The two other storage elements (hot water store and waste water tank) have volumes of 4 m³ and 1 m³.

The electrical power input to the heat pump is 1.2 kW, and the output in the temperature range 15° to 50°C amounts to 3.5 to 4.0.

The main functions of the installation are as follows:

Cooling with the cooling-capacity of the soil (summer).
Heating with solar energy.
Hot water production by solar energy.
Hot water production from waste water by heat pump.
Ventilation with recovered heat.
Heating with soil heat pump.

Figure 9.7
In the Philips experimental energy house, tubular elements are made up in 18 solar panels

In the roof space of the house are two Philips process controllers (P855) for the control of the energy system, the simulation of the energy consumption of the living area, and for the collection of all measurement data on magnetic tape.

The basic building costs amounted to about 600 000 DM. The three years' research work of this pioneer achievement cost 9.8 million DM. The results of the measurements on this experimental house will be made public, and will have an important influence on future German solar projects.

9.6 Zero Energy House, Copenhagen (Denmark)

Project: Vagn Korsgaard, Torben V. Esbenson.
Built: 1975.

The Zero Energy house built in Copenhagen makes use of the approximately 1680 hours of sunshine per year (Figure 9.8).

The annual heat energy requirements of the well insulated house are 5350 kWh (room heating 2300 kWh, hot water 3050 kWh). The house has a living area of 120 m² and a volume of 300 m³, and has six rooms. The solar collector surface is 42 m² and delivers 9017 kWh of energy annually to the main store which has a volume of 30 m³. Of this energy 25 % is used for space heating, 34 % for water heating and the remaining 41 % is storage loss. The domestic water heating is in a 3 m³ tank. The insulation of the house consists of 30 cm of mineral wool (0.14 W/m²/°C).

Figure 9.8
Zero Energy House in Copenhagen (Denmark 55° 43'N.)
1. Radiation   4. Bedrooms
2. Solar collector, water type (42 m²)   5. Living rooms (total 120 m²)
3. Inside garden   6. Hot water store (total 33 m³)

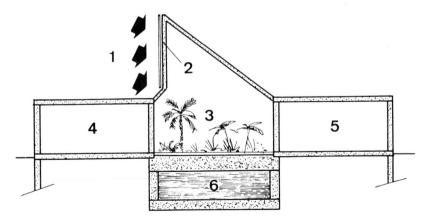

The annual heat requirements of the house are provided by internal heat human (2372 kWh) lighting (2387 kWh) radiation in through the windows (2831 kWh) and solar energy.

9.7 'Solar One House', Delaware (USA)

Project: K. Böer, M. Telkes, K. O'Connor.
Built: 1973.

The solar house of the 'Institute of Energy Conversion' University of Delaware, is claimed to be the first in the world in which the solar radiation, as well as being converted into heat, is also converted directly into electrical power. The building was financed collectively by eight research institutes and electricity supply undertakings. Cost of building, excluding solar cells was 130 000 dollars (Figure 9.9).

Figure 9.9
'Solar One House' in Delaware (U.S.A. 39° 35'N.)

1. Radiation	8. Chemical main store
2. Solar collectors (total 82 m²)	$(Na_2 S_2 O_3 5H_2 O)$ 3600 kg.
3. Thermal buffer zone	49°C, 235 kWh
4. Living space (total 132 m³)	9. Heat pump
5. Return air	10. Electrical suxiliary heating
6. Warm air to living space	11. Accumulator 180 Ah
7. Chemical auxiliary store	12. Installation support
$(Na_2 S_2 O_3 5H_2 O)$	13. Connection to electrical supply

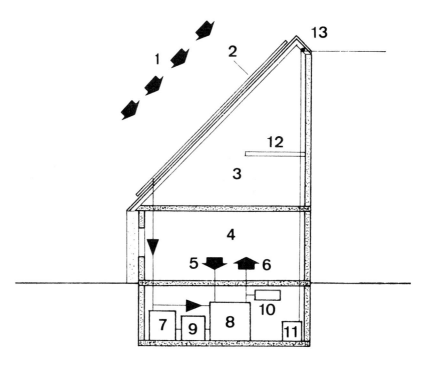

The total living space of the house is 132 m^2; the living rooms are on two levels. The air type solar collectors are mounted on the 45° inclined roof and on the south face. These solar collectors have a total area of 82 m^2, with a double Plexiglass covering. Parts of the solar collectors are combined with solar cells (cadmium sulphide — copper sulphide cells) which have a maximum output of 19 mA/cm^2 at a voltage of 0.37 V. The efficiency of the direct conversion is 6–7 %. The life of the solar cells is estimated at ten years.

The total conversion factor of the collector is 50 %, of which 45 % is converted into heat and 5 % into electrical power. The house receives 80 % of its energy requirements from the sun and the remaining 20 % from electrical power. The heat storage system works on a chemical principle with three different salt solutions which have a low melting point between + 24°C and + 49°C. The heat transfer from collector to store, and transfer from store to the living rooms is by air moved by fans. A heat pump is also associated with the system. The lead/acid accumulators of the electrical storage system have a capacity of about 20 kWh. The solar installation also provides cooling in summer. According to the calculations of Aaron and Isakoff it should soon be possible, through mass production, to be able to make combined solar cells/collectors for 10/m^2 dollars. The chemical heat storage of a similar villa should not cost more than 900 dollars.

Dr. Böer is convinced that before 1980 solar space heating from combined solar cells/collectors will be fully competitive with other heating systems.

Figure 9.10
Desert Research Institute in Nevada (U.S.A. 39° 16'N.)
1. Radiation   4. Buffer zone
2. Solar collectors   5. Laboratory
3. Future collectors

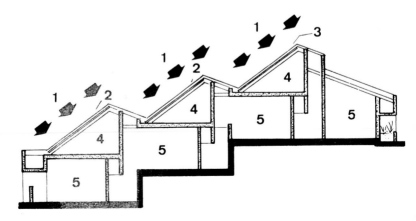

9.8 Desert Research Institute, University of Nevada (USA)

Project: J. Miller Assoc.
Calculations: Arthur D. Little Inc., Johnson-Joeckel, Bartley Assoc.
Built: 1975.

The new biology laboratory of the University of Nevada, receives 50 % of its heating and cooling energy requirements from the sun. In the first building stage, 371.6 m² of surface collectors with selective absorption surface and double glazing are installed.

The cooling system has an absorption installation which functions on the basis of lithium bromide. The inclined building site allows good architectural integration of the solar collectors (Figure 9.10).

9.9 Autonomous Solar House, Cambridge (England)

Project: A. Pike, J. Thring.
Calculations: G. Smith, J. Littler, C. Freeman, R. Thomas.

This solar house project, carried out by a working group of the University of Cambridge, is the result of three years of research work between 1971 and 1974. The result of the study was, that a fully autonomous house with comfort comparable to that which we know today, can be achieved and is also economical.

In this project all locally available sources of energy are utilised. Solar collectors produce heat and distilled drinking water, a wind generator provides electricity for the kitchen,

Figure 9.11
Autonomous solar house in Cambridge (England 52° 12'N.)

1. Radiation	5. Interior garden
2. Solar collectors (40 m²)	6. Living space (total 111 m³)
3. Wind generator	7. Bedroom
4. Hot water store (about 10 m³)	8. Insulating wall to the North

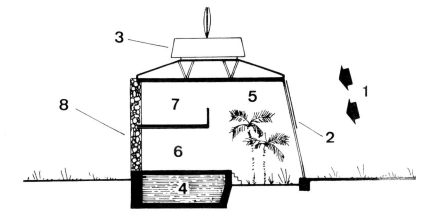

lighting and heat pumps, and the sewage disposal system produces methane. An indoor garden behind the south face produces oxygen and food, and can also be used for most of the year as an 'open space'.

The house has a gross floor area of about 111 m². The living space is on two floors and the garden extends up to the roof (Figure 9.11).

The room heating requires 61 to 75 % of all the energy and uses low grade heat – 50 to 100 W/m² at temperatures between 15° and 30°C. The solar radiation also amounts to a similar value (100 to 150 W/m²). The solar collectors are of surface type and have an area of 40 m².

The heat transfer and storage medium is water. The heat store is in the cellar, and calculations have given an optimum size of 10 m³. In November 1974, a one tenth scale model of the house was produced with which computer simulations are possible to enable optimum dimensions for the units to be determined.

9.10   Dwelling House, Berne (Switzerland)

Project: J. F. Winkler.
Built: 1974.

At this residential site in Berne, a reconstruction programme achieved three times the original building volume.

A heating installation with solar energy was decided upon. The solar collector area is 40 m². On a sunny day about 250 000 heat units are transferred to the store (9000 litres). By extracting 1000 litres per day (45°C) the hot water supply (by solar energy) is guaranteed for a week. By improved insulation, the operating temperature of the existing oil heating installation was reduced from 90°C to 60°C (with an external temperature of 15°C). This allows better use to be made of solar energy. During the summer months and between seasons it is possible to do without the low-efficiency boilers.

9.11   Solar Heated Office Factory, Zurich (Switzerland)

Project: P. R. Sabady.
Calculations: B. Winkler, H. Thomann, R. Aerni, J. Leu.
Completion: 1978.

The building (130 m long, 23 m wide and 25 m high) represents one of the largest buildings in Europe to have provision for the use of solar energy. It is positioned E-W and thus the maximum window area is available on the south side. (See Figures 9.12 to 9.14). This position allows optimum insolation through the south windows in winter, and at the same time affords better protection against summer radiation by means of projecting

Figure 9.12
Project for solar heated office/factory building in Zurich by P. R. Sabady

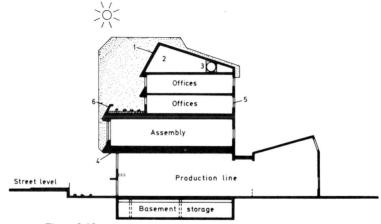

Figure 9.13
Section through the office building
1. Solar panels
2. Thermal insulation zone (air)
3. Heat sink
4. Summer irradiation protector
5. Thermal isolating window
6. Solar panels (later stage)

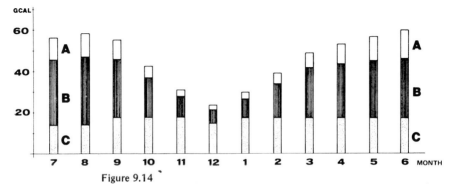

Figure 9.14
'Free Energy' rating (based on calculations by Thomann, Aerni and Leu)
A.   South Face
B.   Solar panels
C.   Internal heating vent

structures. The solar collectors can also be optimally integrated as inclined window frames, roof surface or balconies. At the same time they produce the shade necessary in summer for the window surfaces, and absorb the maximum radiation energy in winter through optimum inclination of 60°. The solar energy from the collectors and south windows is approximately 260 000 Mcal/year and provides part of the heating requirements of the building and hot water for the employees' wash rooms.

To achieve a high collector efficiency a low temperature heating system was selected. Solar energy contributes to the running of the ventilation system. These provisions allow part of the surplus summer energy to be used, whereby about 80 % of the total all round radiation can be utilised.

Heat storage is within the building structure and 75 000 litre water tanks in the roof space. To reduce energy requirements to a minimum, instead of the usual flat roof, a pitched roof is used which makes available storage space for records (archives), an insulated buffer zone, as well as space for heat stores. The windows are fitted with insulating glazing and shutters, and the walls have a good K value of 0.4, to enable the absorbed solar heat to be retained as long as possible. The architectural design allows for the solar collector area to be increased at a later date, when the cost of these components is reduced, and an increased need for cheaper energy arises.

The solar heating installation, which represents about 1.5 % of the building cost, provides annually 100 % of the hot water needs and a significant part of the required space heating energy, whereby at least 230 000 kWh energy can be saved each year.

9.12 Solar heated house in Milton Keynes (England)

Project: Steven Szokolay and the Built Environment Research Group of the Polytechnic of Central London.
Built: 1974

This solar house is a converted local authority house in the new town of Milton Keynes, Buckinghamshire. It was selected to provide an opportunity to examine the economics of application for the mass market. The house is a timber-frame building with lightweight cladding and has been fitted with glass solar panels and aluminium collector plates. Although the insulation of this type of building is reasonably good, the thermal capacity of the building is minimal. The solar system is designed to provide a large part of the energy required for both hot water and space heating. The remaining portion is supplied by conventional means.

A flat plate solar collector was chosen in order to collect the diffuse radiation which comprises approximately 50 % of the total radiation in this country. The chosen house has a roof at a 30° slope which is close to the slope (34°) which gives the yearly

Figure 9.15
The Solar House at Milton Keynes, Buckinghamshire (Milton Keynes
Development Corp.)

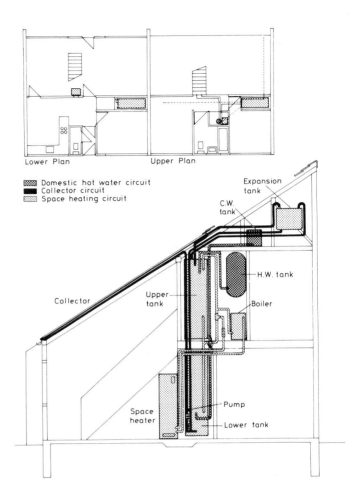

maximum collection. Thus the collector is incorporated into the roof structure, involving few structural alterations.

To reduce the operating temperature of the plate, a direct system was chosen in which the water in the storage tank flows directly through both the collector plates and the space heating unit.

A fan convector unit with increased fin area was chosen, which should give the required heat output for a water inlet temperature of approximately 40°C. By restricting flow through the fan coil, water at 25°C can be returned to the storage, while emitting air at 36°C. Returning water at 25°C to the storage tank helps to reduce the operating temperature of the collector plate, consequently increasing its efficiency. In place of the conventional heat exchanger, a system of small tanks has been used (Figure 9.16).

The water passing through has a long dwell time, approximately eight hours, which should offset the lower heat exchange area. The water than passes to the normal domestic hot water cylinder to

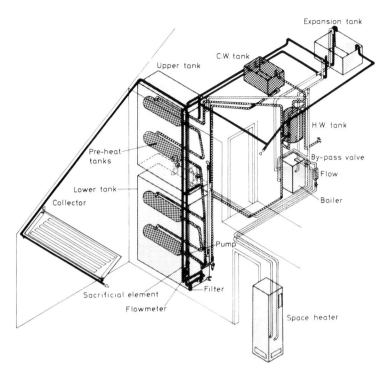

Figure 9.16
Arrangement of collector, domestic hot water and space heating circuits
of the solar house at Milton Keynes (Milton Keynes Development Corp.)

be topped by a conventional immersion heater. This was chosen
in preference to the indirect cylinder, normally fitted in the house,
to facilitate monitoring of the heat supplied to the water and
space heating.

A total of 4.5 m³ (4500 litres) of water storage is used, with
100 mm of glass fibre insulation on all sides. This is equivalent to
120 litres m² of collector area. This volume of water is capable of
storing enough heat for a single day in mid-winter or two days in
spring or autumn. If space had allowed, cylindrical tanks would
have been used at half the cost.

10 Conclusion

In conclusion we would like to quote Prof. P. Fornallaz. In his book 'Technology — for or against Man' he writes:

'Solar energy created the biological basis for human existance. By the realisation of alternative concepts, the technical use of solar energy represents a challenge to the human spirit.

This inexhaustible source of energy appeals also through its social aspect: it is at the disposal of all men, and does not need enormous conversion installations in which the possibility of misuse is inherent, but it stimulates everyone to help himself, and to thrifty self-sufficiency. The social-ethical consideration of the technically possible solutions of the world's energy problem produces the realisation that only the use of solar energy can satisfy technically, economically, ecologically, politically and socially.'

In order to be able to meet this revolutionary technical challenge correctly, the knowledge in this field must be disseminated as widely as possible. The 'Sun Age', as Wernher von Braun correctly named our next century, can only develop through the cooperation of everyone on our Planet.

Figure 10.1
A look into the future with solar panels and wind generator

Appendix 1

Definitions

Additive. In the context of chemical heat storage systems, this is a substance which may be added to other chemicals resulting in a raising or lowering of the temperature at which a change of state occurs.

'Degree Day' concept. As an aid to calculating the heat required to maintain a living space at a desired temperature, in an environment of changing outside conditions, the 'Degree Day' concept is used. The heat required will be equal to the heat lost through the walls to the atmosphere.

Heat lost $= K \times$ surface area $\times$ temperature gradient $\times$ time

where K is the Heat Flow Factor per unit wall thickness as defined below and the temperature gradient is the difference between the inside (room) air temperature and the average outside air temperature (OAT) for the period considered.

By selecting a datum level of average daily OAT of $+12°C$, below which space heating begins and above which heating is no longer required, a 'Heating Day' (HT) is defined as any day when the average OAT is below $+12°C$.

If 'time' in the above equation is reckoned in Heating Days (HT), then to find the heat lost and hence the space heating required for a given period, it is necessary to include a summation of the daily average temperature gradient over the period, thus:

$$\textit{Heat requirement } = K \times \text{surface area} \times \sum_{O}^{HT} (t_i - t_a)$$

The term $(t_i - t_a)$ is called the 'Degree Days' (GT) and represents the sum, reckoned over all the Heating Days of the period, of the measured daily difference between room temperature t_i and the average daily OAT t_a.

Heat pump. To understand the way the heat pump works, it may be considered as a refrigerator which has had its components changed in relative size and located in new positions. Whereas a refrigerator extracts heat from its contents, stored food, in the heat pump heat is extracted from air, water or the ground outside the house. The refrigerator radiates the heat it has extracted from its contents into the room by means of a radiator fitted outside its case; the heat pump radiates the heat it has extracted from the outside source into the living space of the house. Both devices

105

use a refrigeration system comprising pipes, compressor, refrigerant, valves etc.

In a practical heat pump system, for every unit of externally supplied energy used to drive the compressor, about three units of heat energy are obtained: one being the unit put in, the other two being obtained from the outside source — air, river, pond, or ground. The intrinsic design of the heat pump is such that heat is extracted from a low temperature source and delivered at a higher temperature.

Heat conduction. Transfer of heat between particles in solid, liquid and gaseous materials.

Heat convection. Transfer of heat by moving particles of liquids or gases as a result of density change or forced circulation.

Heat radiation. Heat 'rays' are electromagnetic waves which transfer heat between surfaces or between surfaces and their surroundings at different temperatures.

Heat flow factor k. $(kcal/m^2/h/^\circ(C))$. Amount of heat in kcal. which passed in one hour through 1 sq.m. of a structure (e.g. a wall) of thickness d (in metres) in still air when the temperature difference between the air spaces on the two sides (e.g. air in a room and outside air) is $1^\circ C$. (Heat flow normal to the surfaces).

Room air temperature. t_i $(^\circ C)$. This is taken as being the temperature measured at 0.75 m above the floor in the middle of the room, but not further than 2.5 m from the outside walls.

Heat storage capacity. (kcal). Amount of heat taken up in heating a structure, or given out in cooling it.

Specific heat storage capacity = c.y. $(kcal/m^3/^\circ C)$
y = density (kg/m^3)

Specific heat. C $(kcal/kg.^\circ C)$. Amount of heat in kcal which is necessary to raise the temperature of 1 kg of a material by $1^\circ C$.

Heat Conductivity Factor λ. $(kcal/m/h/^\circ C)$. The amount of heat (in kcal) which passes through a 1 m^2 cross section of a uniform material 1 m thick, with uniform heat transfer, when the temperature difference between the surfaces is $1^\circ C$.

Heat Transfer Factor α. $(kcal/m^2/h/^\circ C)$. Amount of heat (in kcal) which is exchanged in one hour between a surface of 1 m^2 and the moving air, when the temperature difference between air and surface is $1^\circ C$.

Heat Storage Factor. Cy. Amount of heat in kcal required to heat 1 m^3 of a body through $1^\circ C$.

Useful equivalents

To melt 1 kg of ice requires	80 kcal
To evaporate 1 kg of water requires	540 kcal
To evaporate 1 kg of alcohol or solvent	100–200 kcal
To heat 1 m^3 air 1°C	about 0.25 kcal
To heat 1 m^3 stone or concrete 1°C	about 500 kcal
To heat 1 m^3 water 1°C	1000 kcal
To heat 1 m^3 brickwork 1°C	about 300 kcal

Heat values

1 kg oil/petrol	10 000 kcal
1 litre (heating) oil, heavy	9300 kcal
1 litre (heating) oil, extra light	8200 kcal
1 kg coal	6000–8000 kcal
1 kg coke	7000–8000 kcal
1 kg 'briquettes'	4000–5300 kcal
1 kg wood	2400–3700 kcal
1 kWh	860 kcal
1 m^3 methane (natural gas)	about 9500 kcal
1 m^3 coal gas	5000–5600 kcal

Derived SI Units

Quantity	Unit	Unit symbol
Force	newton	$N = kg\, m/s^2$
Work, energy quantity of heat	joule	$J = Nm = kg\, m^2/s^2$
Power	watt	$W = J/S = kg\, m^2/s^3$

•

Unit Conversions

$$10^3 \text{ cal} = 1 \text{ kcal (kilo)} = 10^3 \text{ cal}$$
$$\text{(Mega)} = 10^6 \text{ cal}$$
$$\text{(Giga)} = 10^9 \text{ cal}$$
$$\text{(Tera)} = 10^{12} \text{ cal}$$

1 Th	=	25 Mcal (1 therm)
1 kWh	=	860 kcal
1 MWh	=	860 Mcal
1 GWh	=	860 Gcal
1 TWh	=	860 Tcal

Radiation

1 langley $= 1 \text{ cal}/cm^2 = 11.6 \text{ Wh}/m^2$
1 $mWh/cm^2 = 3.17 \text{ BThu/sq ft} = kj/m^2$

Length

1 mm   = 0.039 in
1 m   = 3.28 ft = 1.09 yd

Area

1 m² = 1.196 yd²

Volume

1 m³   = 1.3079 yd³
1 litre = 0.21997 gal

Weight

1 kg   = 0.0197 cwt
1 tonne = 0.9842 ton

Temperature

Celcins (Centrigrade) °C = 5/9 (°F−32)
Fahrenheit   °F = 9/5 (°C) + 32
Kelvin   °K = °C + 273.15

Units of Power are kW, kcal/s, h.p.

1 kW   = 0.239 kcal/s   = 1.36 h.p.
1 kcal/s = 4.1844 kW   = 5.6908 h.p. = 4186.8J
1 h.p.   = 0.17573 kcal/s = 0.73526 kW
1 B.Th.U = 1055J

Units of Energy are kWh, kcal, HPh

1 kWh   = 860.41 kcal   = 1.36 h.p. hour
1 kcal   = 0.00116 kWh   = 0.00158 h.p. hour
1 h.p. hour = 6.23.6 kcal   = 0.73526 kWh

(Stone) Coal Units (SKE)

To compare the energy content of various fuels the average energy content of 1 kg of coal (7000 kcal) is used:

1 kg brown coal	has	0.26 − 0.5	SKE
1 kg peat	has	0.43	SKE
1 kg wood	has	0.5	SKE
l kg oil	has	1.45	SKE
1 m³ town gas	has	0.57	SKE
1 m³ natural gas	has	1.10	SKE
1 kWh	has	0.123	SKE

Appendix 2

Acknowledgements

The author would like to thank the undermentioned firms, institutes, organisations and people who made available data, papers, documents and notes.

Brown Boveri & Co, Mannheim
Philips Research Laboratory GmbH, Aachen
The Minister for Research and Technology, Bonn
Schweizerische Vereinigung für Sonnenenergie, Zürich
Heliosystem, Arcueil
Helibat S. A., Ferrières
Panel Co. Ltd., Tel-Aviv
Aquatic S. A., Paris
Heliothermique, S.A., Mont-De-Marsan
Revere Inc., New-York
PPG-Industries Inc., Pittsburg
General Electric Organisation, Philadelphia
Exenersol, Villeneuve-Loubet
Amcor Export Co. Ltd., Tel-Aviv
Maruo Sangyo Kaisha Ltd., Tokio
Burke Rubber Company, California
Shizuoka Seiki Co. Ltd. Nagoya, Shizuoka
Jetro, Zürich
G. Alexandroff, Paris
J. Michel, Neuilly-sur-Seine
R. Schärer, Grenchen
A. Fischer, Rudolfsetten
P. Valko, Zürich
P. Fornailaz, Zürich
Alcan Aluminium (Europe) S. A., Genf
Liebi, Neuenschwander and Co., Bern
Arbonia AG, Arbon
CNRS, Odeillo
Milton Keynes Development Corporation

ANVAR, Neuilly-sur-Seine
R.T.C., Paris
Arthur D. Little, Inc. Cambridge, Massachusetts
International Solar Energy Society, Parkville, Victoria
Unesco, Paris
GOTO Optical MFG, Co., Tokio
Energie Solaire S. A., St. Sulpice
Grimm & Co., Liebefeld
Miromit S. A., Tel-Aviv
Aquasun France & Coreba S. A., Lyon
Stellar Heat Systems Ltd. (Widmer S. A.), Neuchâtel
Tranter, Inc., Lansing, Michigan
Sofée, Perpignan
German Westlerbureau
A. Stiouim Neuilly-sur-Seine
Elektrizitätsverwertung, Zürich
O. & R. Heim, Zürich
E. Steinacher, Zürich
M. & J. Luif, Uetikon
Dr. I. Orban, Basel
Dr. H. Marhenkel, Mannheim
Dr. Ziegler, Bonn
J. C. Bugnet, Port Marina Baie des Anges
H. Badi, Perpignan
J. Littler, Cambridge
Swiss Meteorological Central Office, Zürich
H. Rüesch, Allenwinden
G. Halasz, Genf
Institute Laing, Aldingen
Swiss Technical Journal, Zürich
Electro-Mechanical Application Ltd

Bibliography

Abetti, G., *The Sun*, Macmillan, New York (1957)

Architectural Forum: *Architecture and Energy*, New York (July/Aug 1973)

Bliss, R. and Bliss, M., 'Design and performance of the Nation's only fully solar-heated house', *Air Conditioning, Heating & Ventilating*, **92**, (Oct 1955)

Böer, K. W., *A combined Solar thermal and electrical house system*, UNESCO Congress, Paris (1973)

Boyle, Godfrey, *Living in the Sun*, Calder and Boyar, London (1975)

Brinkworth, R. J., *Solar energy for Man*, Compton Press, London (1972)

Burnet, F. Macfarlane, 'Winning power from the Sun', *Energy Digest*, (Jan 1973)

Churc, R., Grouch, G. and Vale, B., *'The autonomous servicing of dwellings'* Cambridge (1972)

Curtis, E., 'Rickmansworth House', *Architectural Design* (Jan 1957)

Daniels, F., *Direct use of the Sun's energy*, Yale University Press, USA (1964)

Daniels, F. and Duffie, J. A., *Solar energy research*, University of Wisconsin Press, Madison (1955)

Davies, G. M., 'Model studies of St. George's Wallasey', *Jour. Inst. HVE* **39**, 77 (July 1971)

Davies, G. M., Sturrock, N. S. and Benson, A. C., 'Some results of measurements in St. George's School, Wallasey', *Jour. Inst. HVE* **39** (1971)

Davies, G. M., 'Heating buildings by winter sunshine', *Energy & Housing*, Pergamon Press (1975)

Dietz, A. C. H., 'Large enclosures and solar energy', *Architectural Design* (April 1971)

Dossiers, 'Maisons Solaires', *Techniques & Architecture* (Sept/Oct 1974)

Halacy, D. S., *The coming age of solar energy*, Harper & Rowe, New York (1973)

Hogan, J., 'Solar buildings in the Pyrenees, *Architectural Design* No. 1, London (1975)

Hungerbühler, E., *Energie*, Ravensburger (1975)

Karsgaard, V. and Esbenson, T., 'The Zero Energy house', *Meddelelse* No. 31 (1974)

Kruger, K., *Ingenieure Bauen die Welt*, Safari Verlag (1969)

Lalou, E., *The Sun*, Prentice-Hall, New York (1963)

Loske, *Die Sonnenuhren,* Springer Verlag, Germany (1970)

McLaughlin, T. P., *A House for the Future,* TV Times (1976)

Meinel, A. B. and Meinel, W. B., *Solar energy warm air house heater: Build it Yourself!* Helio Assoc. Inc., Tucson, Arizona (1974)

Michel, J., Vivent, M. and Diament, *Les Maisons Solaires,* Strasbourg (1974)

Moorcraft, C., 'Solar Energy in Housing', *Architectural Design* (Oct 1973)

Morgan, A., 'St. George Wallasey School', *Architectural Design* 10 (1973)

Naegebi, W. N., *Energie,* WWF Switzerland (1974)

Olgyay, A., *Design and Climate,* Princeton University

Olgyay, A. and Telkes, M., 'Solar heating for houses', *Progressive Architecture* (March 1959)

Pike, A., 'Autonomous house', *Architectural Design* (1974)

'Principles of solar house design', *Progressive Architecture* (May 1955)

Rau, H., *Sonnenenergie,* Krausskopf, Wiesbaden (1961)

SSES Handbook (1974 and 1975)

Sabady, P., *Wie kann ich mit Sonnenenergie heizen,* Zurich (1977)

Sabady, P., *Solarbautechnik,* Blauen (1977)

Scharer, R., 'Hallenbad-Becken und Raumheizung mit Sonnenenergie' *Electrizitatscerwertung* No. 3 (1975)

Schriner, R. D. and Cohen, M., 'Bibliography on solar power, *Professional Engineer* (Oct 1973)

Shurcliff, W. A., *Solar heated buildings: A brief survey,* Cambridge University Press (1974)

'Solar air-conditioned house, Brisbane, Australia', *Architecture in Australia* (March 1965)

Solar Energy — A UK Assessment/Report of the UK Sector of the International Solar Energy Society. Published by the Royal Institution in conjunction with the Wolfenden Foundation, London (1975)

Solar heated swimming pool at Westerham, *Architect & Building News* (6/12/67)

'Solar house', *Architectural Design* (Jan 1972)

Steadmann, P., 'Energy Environment', *Building* (1975)

'St. George's School, Wallasey: An evaluation of a solar-heated building', *Architects' Journal* (25/6/69)

Szokolay, S. V., *Solar energy and buildings,* Architectural Press, London (Halstead, USA) (1975)

'The Energy experimental house in Aachen', *Neue Zurcher Zeitung,* No. 150 (1975)

'The Sun in the service of man', *Architects' Journal* (19/8/73)

Thekaekara, M. P., *The energy crisis and energy for the Sun,* Inst. Envir. Sciences, Illinois (1974)

Thomason, H. E. and Thomason, H. J. L., 'Solar house heating and air cooling: Progress report', *Solar Energy* **15** (1973)

Thomason, H. E. and Thomason, H. J. L., *Solar house heating and air conditioning systems*, Edmund Scientific Co., USA (1974)

Trombe, F., *Heating by solar radiation*, submitted from Solar Energy Laboratory, CNRS, France at 1973 UNESCO Conference, Paris

Vale, Brenda and Robert, *The autonomous house*, Thames & Hudson, London (1975)

Valko, P., *Meteoplan*, Hallwag Verlag, Berne (1975)

Vassiliev, M., *'La Conquete de l'energie'*, Editions EM (1971)

Villecco, M., 'Sunpower', *Architektur-Plus* (Sept-Oct 1974)

Watson, D. R. and Barber, E. M. (jr), 'Energy conservation in architecture; Alternative energy sources', *Con.-Arch*, USA (May-June 1974)

Williams, J. Richard, *Solar technology and application*, Ann Arbor Science, London (1974)

Zarem, A. M. and Enway, D. D., *Introduction to the utilisation of Solar energy*, McGraw-Hill, New York (1963)

Zellatt, J. I., 'How materials react to Solar energy: 1 Roofs and walls 2 characteristics of glass and glass shading', *Architectural Record*, (May and June 1966)

Index